Children's Perceptions of Learning with Trainee Teachers

This book is unique as it focuses on pupils' perceptions of their learning with trainee teachers in primary schools. It aims to raise trainee teachers' awareness of the importance of considering pupils' perceptions in evaluating their teaching and provides frameworks for doing so. It enables teachers to make links between theory, research and practice as part of their on-going development.

Includes:

- interviews with primary pupils about their learning with trainee teachers
- examples of new teaching approaches introduced by trainees which are enjoyed and valued by both pupils and mentors
- case studies offering pupil insights into religious education, classroom ethos, gender and ethnicity
- chapter summaries giving suggestions for teaching strategies, discussions with mentors and tutors and further reading

Through interviews, questionnaires, discussion of children's drawings and video tape, a powerful theme emerges. Children like working with trainee teachers. They learn most with trainees who are able to convey key concepts, who stimulate, challenge and change their thinking, who respect them as individuals and maintain a good classroom ethos. This book encourages trainee teachers to develop good practice.

Hilary Cooper is a Principal Lecturer and Head of Programme for Research in Education at St Martin's College.

Rob Hyland was, until recently, a lecturer in education at St Martin's College. Currently he is engaged in a research project at the University of Newcastle.

Children's Perceptions of Learning with Trainee Teachers

Edited by Hilary Cooper and
Rob Hyland

London and New York

First published 2000 by RoutledgeFalmer
11 New Fetter Lane, London EC4P 4EE

Simultaneously published in the USA and Canada
by RoutledgeFalmer
29 West 35th Street, New York, NY 10001

RoutledgeFalmer is an imprint of the Taylor & Francis Group

Typeset in Sabon by
Florence Production Ltd, Stoodleigh, Devon
Printed and bound in Great Britain by
Biddles Ltd, Guildford and King's Lynn

British Library Cataloguing in Publication Data
A catalogue record for this book is available from the
British Library

Library of Congress Cataloging in Publication Data
Children's perceptions of learning with trainee teachers / edited by
Hilary Cooper and Rob Hyland
     p. cm.
   Includes bibliographical references (p.) and index.
   1. Student teachers–Great Britain–Case studies. 2. Education,
Elementary–Great Britain–Case studies. 3. Children–Great
Britain–Attitudes–Case studies. I. Cooper, Hilary, 1943-
II. Hyland, Rob, 1955-
   LB2157.G7 C45 2000
   370′.71–dc21   99-059527

ISBN 0–415–21682–6 PB
     0–415–21681–8 HB

Contents

vi *Contents*

PART III
Do pupils learn what trainee teachers teach?

PART IV
New faces, new ideas?

PART V
Themes, dimensions and issues

Contributors

Charles Batteson is a Principal Lecturer in Education at St Martin's College, working on a range of pre- and in-service teacher-education programmes.

Marion Blake is a Canadian who has lived in England for seven years, the last five in London working as a freelance editor. She was a wandering (postmodern?) graduate student and lecturer at the McGill Faculty of Education, University of London Institute of Education, Ontario Institute for Studies in Education, University of Toronto Faculty of Education and Cambridge Institute of Education. Work as a professional cook enlivened the journey.

Hilary Cooper is Head of Programme for research in education at St Martin's College. Previously she was a lecturer at Goldsmith's College, University of London, an advisory teacher and a class teacher in a variety of London primary schools. She has published widely, largely in the field of history education.

Lorna Crossman is the co-ordinator of primary religious and moral education at St Martin's College; she has also taught in the English Department. Previously she taught in a variety of Birmingham primary schools and was a member of Birmingham LEA Multicultural Development Team. She has particular interests in spiritual development which is not attached to any named religion.

Liz Elliott teaches on education and Information and Communication Technology courses at St Martin's College.

Owain Evans was a class teacher and headteacher before joining St Martin's as a lecturer in Education.

Robin Foster teaches in the mathematics department at St Martin's College. He has taught in a wide variety of situations. His research interests include the development of children's mathematical ideas.

Aftab Gujral is Course Leader for the BSc (Hons) QTS Physical Sciences Course at St Martin's College.

Kevin Hamel is a Senior Lecturer in Music and Education at St Martin's College. He specializes in music and ICT in the primary curriculum.

Maureen Harrison is a Senior Lecturer in Education at St Martin's College and Course Leader of the Year 2 Lower Primary Phase of the BA (QTS) course in Lancaster. Previously Maureen worked in Lancashire primary schools and was Advisory Teacher for Design and Technology in Lancashire.

Mike Huggins is a former head of postgraduate teacher education at Lancaster University. He has spent many years teaching in primary schools and has published widely on educational subjects and nineteenth-century history. He now works as a part-time lecturer and Ofsted Inspector.

Rob Hyland was, until recently, a lecturer in Education at St Martin's College where he taught on Initial Teacher Training and Educational Policy Studies courses. His doctoral research was into the professional first degree.

Kate Jacques is Head of Education at St Martin's where she has been for three years. She taught in primary and secondary schools. She has a particular interest in school culture and the changing nature of teaching as a profession.

Jim Lavin is a Principal Lecturer and Head of the Programme for Physical Education at St Martin's College. His doctoral research investigates the impact of the National Curriculum in this area. He is currently visiting professor at Eastern Connecticut State University.

Suzanne Lea is a Senior Lecturer in the Education Department at St Martin's College. She is Course Leader for Year 2 of the BA (QTS) Programme at the Ambleside campus. Previously she was Head of an Infants Department and a Reception class-teacher.

Jill Pemberton is an artist and teacher. She lectures on Art and Design and Technology courses at St Martin's College.

Anne Riggs is Head of the Department of Science and Technology at St Martin's College. Previously she taught in schools, provided in-service education in biotechnology for teachers in England and Scotland and worked in science education at the University of Surrey.

Florence Down Samson is Co-ordinator of Practicum, Ontario Institute for Studies in Education, University of Toronto, and Field Co-ordinator of the Elementary Central Option. She counts among her experiences of education being the mother of Andrea, Paul and Roger, and being a classroom teacher, a school administrator and a curriculum and programme developer, for the most part in St John's and Cornerbrook, Newfoundland. Her research interests include initial teacher education and the socialization of newly qualified teachers.

Pete Saunders is a Senior Lecturer in ICT. He spent many years teaching in East London Primary Schools and was Regional Coordinator for the National Primary Microelectronic Education Programme.

Neil Simco is a Senior Lecturer in Education at St Martin's College and has responsibility for managing primary partnership with schools. His doctoral research is in the professional developments of teachers.

Nigel Toye is a Senior Lecturer at St Martin's College where he has responsibility for the drama component of all Initial Teacher Training and In-service courses.

Sam Twiselton is a Senior Lecturer in English in primary education at St Martin's College. She teaches on a range of ITT and CPD courses and has special responsibility for English mentor training.

Foreword

Thank heavens for Hilary Cooper and Rob Hyland! They have meticulously edited this book which comes at a most opportune time for all concerned with teacher training and not least the trainee teacher. Over the last ten years school-based pedagogy has increased for students in quantity and indeed some quality as teacher-training establishments come to terms with government strategies and pressures. After more than thirty years of teaching it is very refreshing (if not obvious) for the views of children to be taken into account. How do children perceive the practice of the raw recruit and how does this influence their learning? I should expect this book to be well thumbed and on every trainee's bookshelf.

Graham Fraser
Headteacher
Quarry View Junior School, Sunderland

Acknowledgements

The editors are grateful to all the constituents in the partnership between St Martin's College, Lancaster and the schools in which students on Initial Teacher Training courses are placed, many of whom were involved in the writing of this book.

Since new Partnership arrangements between Teacher Training Institutions and schools became statutory in 1996 teachers have had an increased responsibility for the management, support and assessment of the school-based work of trainees. New courses have been developing and new roles and responsibilities for mentors in schools, for college tutors and also for trainees have been evolving, which aim to develop coherence and shared aims and understandings in supporting the professional development of trainee teachers. These developments have been intended to improve the quality of training, but some teachers have been concerned that their primary responsibility is to teach children. The empirical studies described in this book investigate pupils' perceptions of the impact of trainee teachers on their learning. Children's perception of their learning is often different from that of adults and is often insufficiently considered in evaluating teaching. How can the benefits of working with trainee teachers be maximized and the pitfalls avoided? In a study which reflects and develops new partnership, college tutors, teachers, trainees and their pupils worked together to link theory to practice in investigating these questions.

The editors are grateful to their many colleagues at St Martin's College, those in the Education Department who participated in designing and piloting the initial pupil interviews described in Part I and the generic chapters in Parts II and V and also to the subject application tutors who contributed the case studies in Parts III and IV. Despite very demanding teaching commitments they embarked on each stage of the project with enthusiasm, believed in it, found time to discuss their proposals and findings, met all their deadlines and responded to editorial advice. For this we feel both honoured and grateful. We are especially grateful to Marion Blake for the experience, patience, tolerance, diplomacy, good humour and sheer hard work in her role as editorial adviser, and for widening the scope of the debate by introducing us to her colleague Florence Samson with whom she wrote the afterword.

We are grateful to the teachers and headteachers in our partnership schools throughout Lancashire and Cumbria and in the Isle of Man and Sunderland for their generous professional support of the hundreds of trainees they annually integrate into their school communities, of whom those mentioned in this book form a small random sample. In this instance we appreciate the time spent completing the class-teacher questionnaires and arranging the pupil interviews which underpin the case studies.

We should like to thank the trainee teachers who agreed to participate, accepting that children would comment freely to an interviewer and to college tutors on aspects of their practice not normally scrutinized. And of course we are grateful to the principal contributors to this book, their pupils.

We are very grateful to Susan Cockburn for her patience and efficiency in correcting numerous drafts of the typescript and collating the final version.

For reasons of confidentiality the names of schools, trainee teachers and children have been changed, but they are certainly real places and people in real contexts, as is made clear by the vivid descriptions of situations and vitality of the comments. Throughout the book the terms trainee teacher and student teacher and pupil and child are interchangeable; this is partly for variety and also because sometimes one seems more appropriate than the other depending on the context.

Introduction

Hilary Cooper

'What *is* a student teacher?' a headteacher asked his pupils after twenty-five students had spent an intensive one-week placement working with pupils, teachers and tutors in his school. He received interesting answers.

Student Teachers

Student teachers are half teachers and they help people. In a few years they are real Teachers.
They go to teachers university

When a student teacher is not at school She is in college. She learns how to punish children. She also learns how to learn children, mattes, hangwriting, art, R.e, Reading and English. She learn's the easy way to teach kid's, When, She's in the School She gets influence from the proper teachers.

I think a student teacher takes someone's class so when they get a job in a school they will have some experience with children.

When they are not at school I think they tell there tudor what they done and learned so they can get a job.

When he shared them with the student teachers in a plenary session in college they thought they were hilarious, particularly:

Student teachers, look about the toilets and
go to Classes With Mr fraser.

Yet, on closer scrutiny, there are reflections in these quotations, on the status of student teachers, the length and purpose of a teacher-training course, and of roles and responsibilities in the partnership between the school and the university. It's good to see 'there tudor' still has a significant role. As always with children it is necessary to look beneath the surface statements. For example the ambience of the toilets in this challenging urban school is meticulously nurtured and proudly maintained, with hand cream and scented soap provided for the girls, soccer icons and trophies for the lads, sexist maybe, but this exemplifies the care, respect and creative concern lavished on the school by all who work in it. This remark actually meant that children had noticed that the student teachers, during their brief stay, had acquired some insights into the way in which the ethos of their school was achieved.

What *children* think about working with student teachers was not a dimension to which we had previously given much thought. Mentors in schools are required to take an increasing responsibility for managing, monitoring and assessing the school-based work of trainee teachers, in increasingly circumscribed ways; college courses are increasingly rigorously inspected to ensure that they enable trainees to meet prescribed standards, all with the legitimate aim of enhancing pupils' learning. But, in the midst of all these targets and pressures how do the children perceive their learning with student teachers? After the headteacher had raised the question in a light-hearted introduction to his lecture the question would not go away.

This book evolved over two years. All the contributors are lecturers at St Martin's College. After their initial amusement at the headteacher's quotation they decided to try to find out in more systematic ways, what lay beneath the surface in pupils' perceptions of trainee teachers. The empirical studies through which they did so all took place in schools across Lancashire, Cumbria and the Isle of Man where trainee teachers from St Martin's College are placed as part of the partnership arrangements between schools and the College.

The aims of the book are to raise trainee teachers' awareness of the importance of considering pupils' perceptions in evaluating their teaching; to provide some insights which will maximize the advantages of working with trainees and help them to avoid some of the pit-falls; to investigate a variety of key questions of interest to tutors and students, both generic questions and questions related to teaching subjects across the primary curriculum, in the context of the relevant literature; to provide a range of frameworks which students can replicate, develop or modify to investigate their own practice, as a basis for formal and informal discussions in schools with their mentors, and with college tutors as part of taught courses; to develop coherence both across courses and between schools and initial teacher-training institutions with which they are in partnership. Big aims!

In Part I, The Big Picture, an introductory survey identifies key factors in pupils' perceptions of working with trainee teachers from 130 structured interviews with a random sample of children from Reception to Year 6 taught by trainees from St Martin's College, across Lancashire and Cumbria, in large multi-cultural urban schools, schools in market towns and rural schools with only two classes and two or three teachers. This survey is set in the context of other related studies.

The findings are explained in greater depth in Parts I to V. Parts II and III consist of a series of small empirical studies undertaken by Education and Subject Application Tutors at St Martin's College, investigating questions of interest to them about children's perceptions of their learning with trainee teachers. Each chapter is related to relevant literature and followed by suggestions for investigations student teachers may wish to undertake themselves, questions for discussion with mentors in schools and tutors in college, and recommended further reading.

Part II, Roles and Responsibilities, investigates, through analysis of video clips in Year 6 and children's drawings in Years 1 and 2, how pupils perceive and respond to an additional adult, a student teacher, in their learning environment; how they integrate the new role and the new personality; their expectations and aspirations, and offers some insights into how these can be successfully encompassed. In Chapter 3 Nigel Toye investigates the hypothesis that when the trainee teacher is in a fictional role in drama the power relationship between trainee and pupil is altered; the pupil is unable to rely on the conventional game and has to make sense of the new relationship; this makes real dialogue possible. In Chapter 4 Suzanne Lea explains what children in Nursery and Reception classes think is the teacher's role, how they see the trainee in relation to this role, and how this changes from Year 1 to Year 2.

In Part III, Do Pupils Learn what Trainee Teachers Teach?, case studies investigate, from various perspectives, the factors which influence good match between the learning objectives of the activities trainees plan and children's perceptions of the purposes of these activities in progressing their learning in geography, science, technology, history, English and mathematics.

In Part IV, New Faces, New Ideas?, case studies are used to consider ways in which trainee teachers may introduce new teaching approaches, which are valued by pupils and by their mentors, in art, music, information technology and physical education.

Case studies in Part V explore important cross-curricular themes and issues. Can novice teachers change attitudes in religious education? How do children assess a trainee's ability to control and manage the class? How do children who have never had a male teacher feel about a male trainee? How do children in predominantly white primary schools perceive and respond to black/ethnic-minority trainee teachers; what constructions of race and ethnicity impact on the ways in which they respond and what are the implications for Initial Teacher Training Institutions and the professional support of black/ethnic-minority teachers?

The afterword is written by Marion Blake and Florence Samson. Marion Blake worked with each of the contributors and with the editors from April until September 1999, helping us to turn eighteen discrete papers into a structured book, which we hope has both coherence of style and the varied texture of many voices. Through our regular discussions it became clear that partnership arrangements and responsibility for the professional development of teachers are as much the focus of current changes in her native Ontario as they are in England. Marion Blake and her colleague Florence Samson discuss these connections and the possibilities they offer for new beginnings.

Part I
The Big Picture

1 The Big Picture

What children told us about their work with trainee teachers

Hilary Cooper

'Has anyone – apart from that headteacher in Sunderland – ever asked the *children* what they think about working with trainees?' It was a casual, and possibly facetious aside as we gathered our papers at the end of one of our many Education Department staff meetings in May 1997. We had been discussing, once more, how to develop and refine the ways in which we support mentors in monitoring and assessing trainees' teaching in schools; how to enhance the quality of children's learning with trainees; how to strengthen coherence between work in college and in schools.

'Good question. We don't get into school much to find out any more either ...'
'But it *is* significant isn't it – a fairly *central dimension* in this partnership issue – if you're talking about promoting good teaching and learning – for the children, as well as trainees ...'

People began to shuffle their papers more thoughtfully.

'Do you think we *could* find out more about what children think? Do they *like* working with trainees?'
'Do they think they learn much?'
'What?'
'How?'
'Why?'

Suddenly the calm end-of-meeting atmosphere of professional business successfully completed changed to one of animated questioning and an energetic exchange of ideas. People sat down again.

'We've got £2,000 from the Research Committee for a Partnership Project.'
'Could we do some pupil interviews?'
'No time.'

'We're all visiting a school this term for Postgraduate Link Tutor visits. Could we fit it in then – as a pilot?'

'What is she *on*?' one sceptic enquired at this point.

Nevertheless it was decided that if someone could design an interview schedule, each of us would try it out with at least one group of children during the coming Block Placement, in three weeks time.

That is how our book, *Children's Perceptions of Learning with Trainee Teachers*, began. In fact it is how we, as tutors, really began to work together in a new way, a way which is an on-going part of our work with trainee teachers and their mentors, but which we now approached from a different perspective. In our increasingly busy and circumscribed role as tutors it also enabled us to be creative, to formulate the questions which each of us had been privately pondering for some time, to discuss how we might investigate them in more focused ways, to share the difficulties, to discuss our findings – to talk to *children*! To feel honestly that we are role models of the reflective practitioners we are teaching our trainees to become. For we expect trainees, in discussion with their mentors in school, to analyse the impact of their teaching on children in order to inform their future practice. We as tutors then should find out what *children* say about working with trainees to inform our own course development in College. In doing this we also created a new context for conversations between tutors across education and subject courses.

We even made new professional friends across the Atlantic who became involved in our project! 'It was hard but it was fun' one contributor said recently. But that is to conclude before the project has begun – before our hazy vision slowly evolved into a reality.

First of all, we defined the aims of our study: to provide ideas for trainees towards improving practice; to provide evidence for schools, parents and governors that students are good news; to strengthen the links between college courses and school-based work.

At this stage, May 1997, we planned to write a brief research report of our pupil interviews; perhaps a journal article.

The trailer

Two tutors with some experience of interviewing techniques designed a structured interview schedule which aimed to balance the need for consistency and comparison with an opportunity for open, pupil-initiated responses. We wanted to avoid a series of anecdotes. We also wanted to see whether pupils taught by different trainees, in different schools, would say broadly similar things. After an introductory question encouraging pupils to reflect overall on the work they had done with their trainee they were asked in turn about work in mathematics, English and science – what they had done, learned, enjoyed, found difficult. We focused on the

Core Subjects because all the children interviewed would have spent a significant proportion of time on them, while their experience of the foundation subjects during the placement would have varied. A concluding question was designed to find out about the trainee's contribution to extra-curricular activities and the general life of the school.

As a small addition to their Postgraduate Link Tutor visits sixteen tutors each interviewed a group of three children whom the class teacher felt represented the ability range of their class. Key points made by each of the children interviewed were recorded, verbatim, on a separate response sheet for each question.

The interviews were encouraging. There was much evidence that children felt valued by their trainee teachers and they provided vivid insights into the work they had enjoyed with them – they enjoyed new strategies for learning routine skills: coordinates, 'breaking words into parts', 'learning where commas go'. They also described with enthusiasm a rich variety of more complex learning experiences. At Key Stage 1 these included a Roman feast, making helicopters, boats, musical instruments and space-buggies, experiments with worms and mushrooms, dying and dissecting plants. At Key Stage 2 they talked about gardening clubs, drama, making periscopes and kaleidoscopes and 'examining the organs of a dead sheep'! They enjoyed 'visits' and practical work out-of-doors, often described using specialized language, although this could not be claimed for the five-year-old who 'found out what tadpoles eat – and one jumped out – and I found the difference between poo and their legs'! There were frequent references to trainees 'explaining things well' and much-appreciated individual help. 'When she explains she can tell by the look on your face if you didn't understand. It's like she can read your mind.'

The Big Picture

We were fascinated by the trailer and agreed that we wanted to see The Big Picture – on the wide screen. This time we decided to focus on the pupils taught by undergraduate students on the fourth year of the BA/BSc (with Qualified Teacher Status) course. These trainee primary-school teachers on their ten-week Block Placement are placed in schools across the length and breadth of Lancashire and Cumbria. They are in small rural schools with two or three teachers; schools in market towns from Kendal to Carnforth; big inner-city schools from Carlisle to Barrow, Preston, Blackburn and Burnley. If we interviewed children taught by a completely random sample of trainees across this range of localities and schools would the findings endorse, and strengthen, our pilot study?

The interview schedule, with some minor modifications, had elicited lively and detailed responses. We decided to use our £2,000 to employ Peter Johnson, who had previously been a teacher and who could complete all the interviews during the final eight days of the ten-week placement.

The budget (which included considerable travel costs), allowed him to visit the first, fourth and eighth schools on the placement list for each locality across Lancashire and Cumbria – twenty-five in Lancashire and eighteen in Cumbria. Peter talked to 129 children in groups of three who had been taught by forty-three trainees – that is one-seventh of the total cohort of 301 trainees. Again teachers were asked to select for interview three children, representing the ability range in their class. This was possible in terms of time because the Block Placements in Lancashire were in the Autumn Term, 1997, in Cumbria the following Spring Term, 1998.

In order to add some credence – or otherwise – to the children's perceptions of their learning with trainees, a group of tutors designed a questionnaire for the class teachers. These mirrored the questions asked of the children in the group interviews.

First reel: what the teachers told us

An analysis of the class teacher questionnaires shows that they generally felt that trainees had good subject knowledge both in the core curriculum and in their specialist subjects, that they both successfully promoted and assessed pupils' learning and had a positive impact on pupils' attitudes to learning. This was an encouraging starting point for analysing the pupil interviews.

Second reel: what the children told us

From Reception to Year 6 the children endorsed the findings of the pilot study. As we read and re-read the transcripts we identified four key themes:

1   Children enjoyed 'activities' – doing, making, experimenting, both in and outside the classroom. It seemed that trainees arranged plenty of such opportunities.
2   Children were aware of the ways in which trainees supported their learning, often on an individual basis, through clear instructions, detailed explanations and probing questions.
3   Children felt individually valued by trainees.
4   Children observed, and evaluated, trainees' strategies for creating a purposeful learning environment and making their classroom a good place to be.

It is important of course to recognize that class teachers also provide opportunities for making things, experimenting and work outside school; they too support children's learning and value them! But these were themes the children highlighted in describing their work with trainees. This may be because another adult allocated to work with the class, in addition to the teacher would make it easier to supervise work outside the classroom, to organize out-of-school visits, and to support more complex organizational patterns and learning activities. For in the new partnership arrangements trainees are expected to work in collaborative, team-teaching situations with their peers, class-teachers and mentors, as well as independently. This may also account for the increase in individual attention and one-to-one conversations, both formal and informal, which the children described and valued.

Activities are fun, but what are children learning?

Jean Ruddock, who in a previous study had interviewed secondary-school pupils, found that they responded well to teachers who used 'outings' as starting points for learning (Ruddock 1995). Certainly having a trainee teacher seemed to facilitate 'outings' as part of the curriculum for our primary interviewees. Twenty-seven of the forty-three groups interviewed talked enthusiastically about 'visits' arranged by the trainee – to theatres as a stimulus to their work in drama, to museums and sites related to work in history and to farms, parks, nature-reserves, beaches, markets, shops and power-stations linked to work in science, geography and environmental studies.

In addition to 'visits' most of the children described activities in which they had participated; things they had made; investigations and experiments, with constant references to 'fun', 'exciting', 'enjoyment' and 'very interesting'. These are all the kinds of work which allow children and teachers to get to know each other.

But more importantly these vivid recollections, recounted with enjoyment, also suggest that, although the children may have perceived them as simply coinciding with their own interests, they were also learning what the trainee intended to teach. This corroborates the research of Paul Cooper and Donald MacIntrye who found that when children remember key events in their learning with pleasure this implies 'cognitive stimulation' and that as a result the teacher's learning objectives were generally achieved. (Cooper and MacIntrye 1993).

Indeed children often made it clear that they had understood the learning objectives of an activity, generally considered an accurate indicator that they achieved them. Five-year-old Ahmed described how 'we tested things like toast and ice to see if they would go back to normal', and Daniel aged seven knew that he was learning about measurement of length when they 'had competitions and had to be a frog and measure how far you could jump'. 'Games make work more fun', he explained.

Sometimes children may have felt that they set their own learning objectives but the trainee clearly shared their agenda! Emily, aged eight, liked working with the trainee because 'she lets us do what *we* want to do'. It transpires that what Emily and her class wanted to do above all was . . . to make electrical circuits. 'It was great', she said. 'We learned a lot about symbols and conduction.'

The words children used also implied that they understood what they were expected to learn through the activities. Jody, aged five, 'heated salt crystals to see how they would change – it's like experimenting'. Peter, at ten, found setting up a newspaper, which involved 'lots of English', very much in line with his future plans to be a journalist: 'deconstructing stories, considering reports from various points of view, questioning local people in order to collate information'.

The common features of the enjoyable activities which the children described were that they were usually new to them, were collaborative, had a product, and involved participation, decision-making and choice.

Instructions, explanations, questions: was learning sufficiently progressed?

Most of the children then seemed to learn while being taught by trainees and to enjoy learning, but were they sufficiently challenged? A third of the children interviewed spontaneously associated 'hard work' with 'fun' and 'interesting'. Craig, aged seven, said that things are hard 'but she makes it fun – interesting' and Ryan, also seven, said that 'Mr Jones makes maths good. Volume and capacity are very hard but he helps us – makes it fun'. Eleven-year-old Nicola said, 'Miss Lambert pushes us in maths and she gives us challenging tasks in English. We like it.'

Hard work is associated with fun when pupils understand (Cooper and MacIntyre 1993). Our enquiry supports this common-sense observation. The children talked about ways in which trainees helped them to understand. They talked about clear instructions. Hayley (aged ten) said that, 'he explains what he wants you to write. You have to listen carefully. He often starts you off. Then you have to work it out.' They talked about trainees who explained work well. 'She gives us hard work but she explains it in detail; makes it clear – exciting.' Children were made aware of their progress. 'He helps us *see* what we're learning.'

Children were also aware of trainees who recognized their different levels of understanding, and when they as individuals needed help, who matched work appropriately and took the trouble to explain it further.

> We made newspapers in English. She makes you work it out. She only helps you if it's really hard and you get stuck. Maths is my best subject. We do lots of hard work and I know lots of things. If you're sucking your fingers she knows you're stuck and comes and helps. She helps you get it right. She can show us on her fingers how to do it. She's very practical.
>
> Danny, aged six

Only one group of children (ten-year-olds), was critical of their trainee teacher, making the salutary observation that:

He always starts shouting at us when he's trying to explain things. All his questions were as someone who is exasperated. He makes it far harder. He always explained things in science in such a way that they were harder to understand. In art he didn't give us much to do, and when we'd finished we just had to read. Generally he explained what it means but not how to do it, then he said, well – I've explained – you should know.

Developing relationships and self-esteem: what did children value?

One of the qualities children cherish in teachers, as do we all, is a sense of humour. In the relatively short time that trainees had with their classes, and with so much for them to achieve and to demonstrate in order to pass the placement, could they dare to risk humour? Over the ten-week placement did they begin to belong, to gain confidence, to relax into being themselves? Some certainly did, and the children, across the age-range, acknowledged this.

> We did jokes with her. We all had our own joke to tell.
>
> Grant aged five.

> She has lots of funny ways. She sometimes makes funny songs up . . .
>
> Amy aged seven.

> She's funny; she's generous. She has a giggle with us and the work is always more fun.
>
> Lucy aged ten.

> She's humorous – but she sorts things out.
>
> Andy aged eleven.

The Year 5/6 class taught by Mr Woods missed out somehow.

> He didn't make jokes. He didn't understand us. He didn't encourage us at all.

Children talked about trainees who were approachable, who trusted them and formed relationships with them. Steven said that Miss Grey in his Year 2 class, '*helps* us do things. She doesn't *make* us'. Darren, in Year 5, said that people like stopping behind to help Mr Hill and that he always had a job for them. 'Having a job makes you feel he can trust you. In lessons he picks out *positive* people, to show how good they are', and in Year 6, 'Miss Johnson is someone you can *talk* to. We help her with the displays, and talk to her. We like her a lot.'

The children liked trainees who got to know them quickly as individuals, found ways of showing that they liked them and delighted in their progress. Miss Johnson in Year 1 knew that Tim was particularly good at sorting things and – amazingly – constantly found, 'things which needed sorting', which pleased Tim tremendously! Miss Fox in Year 3, 'had a good understanding of our temperaments'. Miss Jackson made pupils in Year 4, 'confident about doing things', while Mr Williams in Year 6, 'noticed when children did well and was always pleased when they got things right'. Children liked trainees who found ways of showing that they valued not just individuals but also the class as a whole. Miss Bower liked her Year Two class so much that she, 'even went home and told her friends how good we are and showed them our good work, and they were amazed that we could do it'.

Keeping the classroom a safe, productive place; pupils' perspectives

Bronwyn Davies (1982) observed and interviewed a class of ten-year-olds over a year as they coped with a succession of three teachers with very different teaching styles. These children had learned that school is about pleasing adults and had developed many skills to enable them to do so. They accepted explicit surface ground-rules set up by each new teacher while they learned the more complex interactional rules for getting on with each of the teachers. These can only develop over time. When the rules broke down they tried to work out why. The most successful of the three teachers was Miss Love who took full responsibility for framing and carrying out her own agenda, but in doing so had an intuitive grasp of the pupils' perspectives. Once the ground-rules were clear and perceived to be fair, children accepted them. Then it became possible to establish more subtle rules for relating to each other over time. Once the children understood how these worked Miss Love could do no wrong.

The pupils interviewed in our study were similarly observant and tolerant in accepting a trainee's initial, short-term behaviour management strategies. In Year One they were aware that 'little sums help you to wait quietly when you're lining up for play'. In Year 5 they knew that, 'reading to us while we're working stops us talking', and that, 'he taught us sign language so we don't make a noise'. They went along with the introduction of new punishments, (naughty boards, traffic-light warning systems), and with new rewards systems, (prizes, star charts, certificates). One class was rewarded with dragon food; 'He gives out dragon food instead of house-points – he's Welsh'.

Meanwhile children were watching and evaluating attitudes and values underpinning these systems. They talked about firmness, fairness, quietness and good humour.

She's firm, but not unnecessarily strict. She lets you off if you're repentant.

> Jodie, aged nine.

She's kind, but not soft. She's strict enough. She treats everyone with respect. She's always fair. She stops us going over the top . . .

> Sam, aged eleven.

A third of the groups interviewed talked about shouting, which they hated. They also disliked 'moods'. Although Miss Hughes did 'exciting stuff' with her Year 4 class her inconsistent moods were noted. With older pupils fairness was often talked about with references to gender.

She's the same with the boys and the girls; the boys cause more trouble generally – but she can handle them.

> Sally, aged ten.

He couldn't control us. He never kept his word on punishments. He was only nice to us when we were nice to him. He always picks boys to help the girls. When he's angry it's always with the boys. He never shouts at the girls.

> Dean, aged eleven.

Four-year-old Sally, who has only been in school for three weeks but is already acutely aware of roles and hierarchies, occupies the last frame of the Big Picture.

Miss Newman is like a real teacher. She sits in the rocking chair at story time. The parent helpers just sit at tables.

The first screening

But this was not the end. The Big Picture was shown to a larger group of tutors from subject departments as well as those in the Education Department, on a college-wide education research day. Discussion generated further questions. Children may often have *seemed* to share trainees' learning objectives, but how closely, and in what circumstances? How was this related to the quality of instructions, explanations, questions, interactions? What did children respond to best in particular subjects and why? Can we find out more about their perceptions of 'fairness'; about how to move from basic ground rules for behaviour to establishing good ethos and relationships? How do pupils perceive trainees in relation to all the other adults working in schools and the continuity in their learning?

The project group grew. During the following term, Summer 1998, education and subject tutors met to plan a series of small-scale empirical case studies, through which they could investigate these questions in more depth during the next Final Block Placement, in Spring 1999, as part of their Quality Assurance visits to see how their subject is taught in schools. The credits roll. The title appears on the screen, 'Children's Perceptions of their Learning with Trainee Teachers . . .'.

Back to reality: the book

By now we had begun to think that this project might not be just of interest to us, as an aspect of evaluating our courses. Surely the people who would most want to know what children say about trainee teachers are . . . trainee teachers. How can you fit comfortably into class routines, and also make your own contribution about things which passionately concern you, as an art specialist perhaps? How can you avoid at least some of the difficulties and get the children on your side in subjects where you are not a specialist and may be less than confident, perhaps in music, or history or Religious Education? Do children really learn the things you hope and plan to teach them?

Rob Hyland and I were asked to contact the commissioning editor at Routledge, with whom I had worked on another occasion, with a proposal for . . . A BOOK. The proposal was sent to three readers for comment. The first said:

> This is a timely proposal. Increased contact time and emphasis on primary trainees' direct teaching in schools has heightened the general level of interest in their work. This book may well identify a range of benefits not always apparent to teachers in working with trainees and suggest to trainees ways of improving their practice. Judicious use of children's opinions should further enhance it. From the style of the proposal the book should be interesting and lively . . .

The second:

> This looks a very interesting and worthwhile book. It will be of interest to trainee teachers and all those involved in their training. . . . At the moment there are endless books about mentoring but I am not aware of any books which report on children's experience of working with trainee teachers. . . . I very much like the proposed style of the book. . . . Trainees often lack the every-day experience in classrooms to understand points made at too abstract a level and children's comments will be very positive in this regard . . .

However, the third said:

As it currently stands it reads as a set of ideas which are still in need of some fine-tuning, and which as yet seem to lack a theoretical base . . .

So, we firmed up our proposal. Each of the contributors identified a key question concerning children's learning with trainee teachers in their area of subject specialism and explained how they would investigate it, and link it to the existing research accounts, through a small-scale study based on observations and discussions with children in classrooms. 'Fine', said the editor, when she came to meet us in college just before Christmas 1998, 'but how can trainees *use* this analysis to improve their practice?'. So after two hours of intense discussion we agreed that each chapter would end with suggestions for ways in which readers could use the case study as a framework or a starting point for finding out what *their* pupils thought about *their* teaching, as a basis for discussion with their mentors in school, and their tutors in college. A multi-faceted reflection on practice!

We all signed our contracts in January and made arrangements to begin our work in schools.

Suggestions for:

Student investigations

Involve the children in your interim or summative evaluation of a Block Placement in School. Find out what they particularly enjoyed, found new or difficult in the work they have done with you. With younger children this could be in a circle time. With older pupils this could be done in a Literacy Hour on non-fiction. In the introduction the whole class could read an outline of one of your medium-term plans, on a flip chart or overhead transparency, discussing headings, bullet points and sequence of work. In small groups they could discuss for example what they have enjoyed most, found new, found difficult, possibly recording key points. In the plenary these could be collated using headings and bullet points.

Discussion with mentors in school

- As part of an interim or summative tutorial discuss aspects of the children's evaluation. Are there new insights? Does the mentor agree? What are the explanations; implications for future action plans?

Discussion on college-based courses

- Focus on and critically analyse a significant incident mentioned by the children, and discussed with your mentor. What caused it? How will this analysis inform your subsequent professional development?

References

Cooper, P. and MacIntyre, D. (1993) 'Commonality in teachers' and pupils' perceptions of effective classroom learning', *British Journal of Educational Psychology* 63, 381–399.

Davies, B. (1982) *Life in the Classroom and Playground: The Accounts of Primary School Children*, London: Routledge, Kegan and Paul.

Ruddock, J., Chaplain, R. and Wallace, G. (eds) (1995) *School Improvement: What the Pupils Tell Us*, London: David Fulton.

2   Why children's perceptions?

The context for the inquiry

Rob Hyland

Hilary has described how *Children's Perceptions of Learning with Trainee Teachers* arose out of the shared interest of a group of tutors in investigating the pupils' learning during their time with teachers from St Martin's College. Our central and unifying concern was the relationship of children's learning to student teachers' teaching, seen within the context of developing partnerships between schools and higher-education institutions. In this chapter I set out the broader context in the changing institutional arrangements for initial teacher education and the wider debate on pupils' perceptions of their learning.

Partnerships for learning

How teachers should best be educated and trained has been argued about for as long as there has been a school system. Almost every inquiry into initial teacher training has discussed the appropriate proportion of time to be spent in schools (often labelled as *teaching practice* or *teaching experience*) and in colleges and universities. In the long history of training teachers in the United Kingdom, the policy pendulum has swung back and forth. Many other countries can demonstrate a similar pattern of policy shifts: more practical work in schools; then more instruction in institutions of higher education; then once more in favour of increasing the contribution of practical work in schools. In a speech to the North of England Education Conference (4 January 1992), the UK Secretary of State for Education, Kenneth Clarke, signalled the main principle for changing policy in the 1990s:

> Student teachers need more time in classrooms guided by serving teachers and less time in the teacher-training college.
>
> (Clarke 1992 para 19)

Translated into specific policies and regulations, this principle was to have major implications for courses of initial teacher-training (ITT) at institutions such as St Martin's College.

What was proposed was more than simply an increase in the time trainees spend in schools: government measures to make the initial preparation of would-be teachers more effective would involve the creation of new understandings and 'a more equal partnership' between higher-education institutions (HEIs) and schools. Though there was resistance amongst some HEIs to proposals which would transfer a proportion of power and financial resources to schools, and some understandable scepticism about the political rhetoric of the language of 'partnership', this term came to characterize ITT in the late 1990s. Though initially impelled by government directives, circulars and guidelines, ITT institutions come to build positively upon the notion of a 'partnership' between schools and higher education. There is widespread agreement that the effective training of teachers does indeed require close links between school-based and HEI-based elements with full recognition of the role of all the partners in this relationship. Tutors at St Martin's College and heads and teachers in schools continue to work towards an effective, closer and constantly developing partnership for teacher training.

That a closer partnership between ITT and schools is likely to provide more effective learning for trainee teachers is sensible enough. That trainee teachers need time in classrooms in order to develop the practical skills of their chosen career may be self-evident. That higher education institutions running courses of teacher training need access to school placements for their student trainees is a logical consequence. But what of the interests of the various stakeholders in this? What can a closer involvement in partnership with ITT institutions bring to schools? What will partnership relationships mean for teachers, tutors and trainees? And the focus of this book, what does the partnership model mean for pupils?

The importance of induction into the profession of teaching, its knowledge and skills, is universally recognized. As Crowther's examination (1995) of a primary-school view of involvement in ITT suggests, teachers recognize that part of their professional responsibility is to contribute to the induction of trainees into the values and practices of teaching. Derek Haylock's small-scale study (1994) of why primary schools in East Anglia accept trainees found that contributing to the preparation of those in training is one way in which teachers demonstrate a sense of belonging to a profession with an identity, a set of values and concerns beyond the immediate present. Our experience at St Martin's confirms these findings: in welcoming trainees, it is clear that teachers, heads and governors of schools are committed to the professional development of students and newly qualified teachers.

Though providing practical opportunities and support for trainees as they learn makes considerable demands on schools, it does have immediate benefits. Most trainees bring great enthusiasm and commitment to their classroom work, as well as knowledge and skills. As a headteacher in Haylock's study (1994: 70) commented: 'It's not just an extra pair of hands. As someone once said, the extra pair of hands comes with a free brain'. Our inquiry was in part driven by an interest to discover just what those 'free brains' did contribute. We wanted to know the benefits such an involvement with trainees had for the pupils. Whilst (at least for those of us directly involved in institutions of ITT) asking this question may seem like an attempt to justify the demands made of schools for trainee placements, it is an important question for all the partners. We are all concerned that whilst in schools trainees should have a positive impact upon the learning of the pupils. More directly still, our inquiry asked: What sense do pupils make of their work with trainees? What do *they* think they have learned? What difference has the presence of trainees made for *them*?

Asking the learners

Why concern ourselves with pupils' perceptions? Within these new partnership arrangements we increasingly knew a good deal about what teachers and headteachers thought about the work of our students. We also certainly knew what government inspectors from the Office for Standards in Education (Ofsted) thought. And of course we had our own sense of what students contributed both to schools and to pupils' learning. But why ask *children*?

One phrase from the Plowden Report on primary education (1967) has probably been cited above all others: 'At the heart of the educational process lies the child'. Once quoted so approvingly as a key statement of progressive practice, it has subsequently been much mocked as the rather naïve slogan of child-centred education. But mockery is not the same as refutation. Provided it is understood that, while primary education necessarily has children at its centre, it does not simply accede to the children's immediate interests and desires but actually requires planned, purposeful and knowledgeable teaching, then a more serious and helpful reading of this statement can be offered. *Children's Perceptions of Learning with Trainee Teachers* assumes that pupils (students at any stage) are indeed at the centre of educational processes, and that there are both ethical and pragmatic imperatives for actively seeking the learners' views and understandings.

The ethics of taking pupils' perspectives seriously raises complex issues and a few key points should be kept in mind. If, as so many of our statements of educational aims in democratic societies claim, our long-term intentions are to develop pupils as independent learners, informed and autonomous agents able to think about and act upon the issues of the day, then we should provide sustained opportunities for them to consider their own learning in school. Taking children's views into account raises a challenge: clearly pupils are not in a position to understand the causes, motives and implications of the teaching for them. But serious examination of learners' perspectives can be an antidote to some of the more simplistic romanticism about the wisdom of the child. Children's judgements are often acute, but some things may be too far beyond their present experience and maturity to appreciate. It seems to me that the ethical position is that pupils have a right to have their observations and opinions taken seriously, though I am not suggesting that we rely on them as the final judgement on the teaching they receive.

Matters of principle and pragmatism meet when it is recognized that pupils can actively contribute to teachers' developing skills and professional knowledge. The practical justification for enquiring into pupils' perspectives is that their ideas on their school experience are directly relevant to developing more effective teaching. As Hayes observes:

> Teachers who make a habit of asking children their views are often surprised by the perceptiveness of their comments. Any evaluation of school effectiveness is enhanced by asking those most intimately involved in the process.
>
> (Hayes 1996: 2)

Again, pupils have a contribution to make as partners in the search for educational improvement. Pupils are indeed often more self-aware and able to reflect upon their experiences as learners than may be commonly assumed:

> Children reveal that they have the articulateness and honesty to analyse what they experience. They show consistent judgement and evidence for what they are saying. Their views deserve to be taken into account because they know better than anyone which teaching and learning styles are successful, which techniques of learning bring the best out of them and what the ethos of the school consists of . . . listening to children makes us consider some of the habits we have taken for granted.
>
> (Cullingford: 1991: 2)

Considering taken-for-granted habits is central to developing a reflective and evaluative approach to teaching. But how can trainee teachers acquire the skills of reflecting upon and evaluating their classroom practice? What exactly is to be reflected upon? Trainee teachers can learn to collect and use direct and indirect evidence of pupils' experience and perceptions as part of a constant check on the relationship between what they intended to teach and what the children have learned. That the professional development of both qualified and trainee teachers ought to be focused upon the promotion of pupil learning may seem to some to be self-evident; what is being argued beyond this, however, is that beginning teachers should seek to enquire *actively* into their pupils' perceptions of the lessons.

This is the rationale of the book. Our purpose was not simply to report studies of the impact of trainees upon pupils' learning, but also to advance the case for trainees to investigate the perceptions held by pupils. This approach has to be viewed within a developing research literature that sees this focus as an important perspective on teaching and a contribution to the development of trainee teachers' professional knowledge and skills.

Examining pupils' perceptions

Since the 1960s, there have been many studies seeking to investigate pupils' experiences in the classroom. One of the classic American examples of an observational study is Philip Jackson's *Life in Classrooms* (1968). In this he sought to explain many routine classroom activities in terms of the meanings pupils assigned to them, rather than the explanations given by teachers. Jackson pointed out, for example, that pupils are often reacting to the 'hidden curriculum' rather than the formal curriculum; they may be more preoccupied with avoiding public criticism than with reaching the academic objectives identified by their teacher. The implications for teachers were that they should not immediately assume that the lesson's purpose is necessarily understood or shared by pupils and must seek to uncover pupils' perspectives on classroom events.

Participant–observer studies, in which the researcher works closely with or as a teacher rather than attempting to maintain a 'neutral' observer position, include those of Armstrong (1980), Rowland (1984) and Pollard (1985). All offer illuminating accounts of primary-school life, closely observed and recorded in different ways. Whereas Pollard's study concentrated on pupils' coming to terms with the social world of the school, Armstrong and Rowland are both full of insights into children's learning in the classroom. Michael Armstrong focused very clearly on the development of individual pupils' 'intellectual growth'; he tried to explore what lay behind changes pupils made in their work with many detailed accounts of how a single child developed a particular picture or story. Stephen Rowland extended this approach and argued in *The Enquiring Classroom* for a model of 'interpretative' teaching which required continual, careful investigation of children's developing understanding so that teachers' interventions would have a positive effect in fostering pupils' personal sense of learning.

Many studies have attempted to uncover the developing understandings of pupils as they come to terms with particular aspects of the social and academic aspects of school. The collection of articles edited by Andrew Pollard *Children and their Primary Schools* (1987) focused largely on the socio–cultural aspects of pupils' experience. Margaret Jackson (1987) examined how young children first started 'making sense of school'. Lee *et al.* reported on some evidence of children of the nine- to eleven-year-old age-group developing perceptions of race, class and gender. More recently, researchers have incorporated pupils' perspectives into studies of the effects of legislative change in the UK. In a study evaluating the impact of major reforms of education upon Key Stage 1, Pollard *et al.* (1994) looked at pupils' attitudes to school as a contribution to the overall picture. West *et al.* (1997) investigated the attitudes of children aged six to seven to the subjects of the National Curriculum. What characterizes such studies is the wish to go beyond the immediately observable overt behaviour or recorded academic performance of pupils and actively to seek out their underlying concerns and patterns of thinking. The argument is simple: to evaluate change in education requires close attention to the experiences of learners and the meaning events and practices have for them.

Children's Perceptions of Learning with Trainee Teachers does not aim to develop new theory or a fully articulated model of teaching and learning, nor is it a systematic introduction to pedagogical principles or a general guide to learning to teach. What the chapters which follow offer are examples of studies which we hope will encourage others – especially trainees – to reflect further on their practice and to investigate actively pupils' perceptions. That teachers and would-be teachers should reflect on their practice has become an orthodoxy; this book suggests some issues for reflection. The central argument remains: in order to advance pupils' learning, teachers should consider what do pupils' perceptions have to tell us of their learning experiences? The message from the contributors to trainees is direct: investigate what children have to tell you and reflect on your teaching in the light of what you find. Our responsibility as tutors is to model, demonstrate and assist in this process.

Points for discussion

'The Word for Teaching is Learning' (title of M. Lightfoot and N. Martin's book published in 1988); 'nothing's been taught till it's been learned'; 'teaching and learning are two halves of one verb' – these are all variants of a time-honoured piece of advice for beginning teachers. What point is being made here? What are its implications?

Asking pupils to reflect on their experiences in school can present some dilemmas. There are practical and ethical questions in canvassing pupils' opinions. There is always a problem with asking pupils questions which, if only indirectly, may tend to invite invidious comparisons of other teachers. This is a more important point than is often recognized: it is illuminating of a more general problem of knowing how to acknowledge and utilize responses from pupils about their experience of the processes of teaching and learning. What ethical and practical considerations should we take into account when enquiring into pupils' perceptions of their learning?

Cognitive processes are not available for immediate inspection and there are obvious difficulties in accessing and interpreting pupils' perceptions of their learning. This is partly a matter of fostering a willingness in pupils to disclose their ideas, but can this be taught as a practised skill? How might the conscious reflection of 'metacognition' be encouraged? How can we best incorporate into our teaching what we learn from pupils about their learning?

Suggestions for:

Further reading

For what still remains a most illuminating study of the unintended as much as the intended effects of teachers' work in classrooms see: Jackson, P. W. (1968) *Life in Classrooms*, New York: Holt, Rinehart & Winston.

Despite the date of publication, many of the insights are so acute as to remain timeless.

For a more recent examination of pupils' perspectives on the primary or elementary school curriculum in Canada and the USA as well as the UK see: Pollard, A., Thiessen, D. and Filer, A. (eds) (1997) *Children and their Curriculum: The Perspectives of Primary and Elementary School Children*, London: Falmer Press.

As well as examples of studies of children's perspectives, this also contains three chapters which discuss some of the methodological issues involved.

For a collection of articles applying constructivist perspectives to the primary curriculum see: Littledyke, M. and Huxford, L. (eds) (1998) *Teaching the Primary Curriculum for Constructive Learning*, London: David Fulton.

The two introductory chapters by Michael Littledyke provide a very readable introduction to constructivist ideas and their implications for teaching. Subsequent chapters discuss how pupils construct their learning in different subjects of the primary curriculum.

For a thorough investigation of psychological aspects of learning in classrooms, with extensive treatment of the ideas of Bruner and Vygotsky and detailed discussion of the significance for teachers of how pupils approach their learning, see: Tharp, R. G. and Gallimore, R. (1988) *Rousing Minds to Life: Teaching, Learning and Schooling in Social Context*, Cambridge: Cambridge University Press.

Though this is quite a demanding book to read, Tharp and Gallimore do develop a model of teaching which is both grounded in a well-researched theory of pupils' learning and suggests how teachers can actively assist this further.

References

Armstrong, M. (1980) *Closely Observed Children: The Diary of a Primary Classroom*, London: Writers and Readers.

Bruner, J. (1966) *Towards a Theory of Instruction*, Cambridge, MA: Harvard University Press.

Crowther, G. (1995) 'A primary school view of involvement in initial teacher training', in H. Bines and J. Welton (eds) *Managing Partnerships in Teacher Training and Development*, London: Routledge.

Cullingford, C. (1991) *The Inner World of the School*, London: Cassell.

Hayes, D. (1996) *Foundations of Primary Teaching*, London: David Fulton.

Haylock, D. (1994) 'The extra pair of hands comes with a free brain', in I. Reid, H. Constable and R. Griffiths (eds) *Teacher Education Reform: Current Research*, London: Paul Chapman Publishing.

Jackson, M. (1987) 'Making sense of school', in A. Pollard (ed.) *Children and their Primary Schools: A New Perspective*, Lewes: Falmer Press.

Jackson, P.W. (1968) *Life in Classrooms*, New York: Holt, Rinehart and Winston.

Lee, V., Lee, J. and Pearson, M. (1987) 'Stories children tell', in A. Pollard (ed.) *Children and their Primary Schools: A New Perspective*, Lewes: Falmer Press.

Lightfoot, M. and Martin, N. (eds) (1988) *The Word for Teaching is Learning: Language and Learning Today: Essays for James Britton*, London: Heinemann Educational.

Plowden Committee (1967) *Children and their Primary Schools* (Report of the Central Advisory Council for Education, The Plowden Report), London: HMSO.

Pollard, A. (1985) *The Social World of the Primary School*, London: Holt, Rinehart and Winston.

Pollard, A. (ed.) (1987) *Children and their Primary Schools: A New Perspective*, Lewes: Falmer Press.

Pollard, A., Broadfoot, P., Croll, P., Osborn, M. and Abbott, D. (1994) *Changing English Primary Schools?: The Impact of the Education Reform Act at Key Stage 1*, London: Cassell.

Rowland, S. (1984) *The Enquiring Classroom: An Approach to Understanding Children's Learning*, Lewes: Falmer Press.

Vygotsky, L. S. (1962) *Thought and Language*, trans. E. Hanfmann and G. Vakar, Cambridge, MA: MIT Press.

West, A., Hailes, J. and Sammons, P. (1997) 'Children's attitudes to the National Curriculum at Key Stage 1', *British Educational Research Journal*, 23(5): 597–613.

Part II
Roles and responsibilities

3   Drama

Pupils' perceptions of the power game

Nigel Toye

> We don't trust ourselves and our pupils to develop working rela-
> tionships whereby [pupils] can assume real responsibility within the
> system. Teacher dependence, if not necessarily overt, is still a covert
> factor. I would hope that no teacher would deliberately set out to
> keep their charges in thrall to them. The problem lies with the trailing
> encumbrances attached to the role of *student* [pupil] when linked with
> the word teacher. . . . It establishes a mind set.
>
> (Heathcote 1998: 3)

Dorothy Heathcote is one of the most influential drama practitioners this
century. She continues to teach us how to use powerful symbols and
strong material to grapple with big issues. She does this by weaving the
basic elements of theatre into our subject teaching.

She has always seen herself as a teacher first and as a drama teacher
second. Drama is at the centre of the curriculum and can provide the
focus for subject work over several weeks.

Dorothy's major contribution to current practice was her introduction
of teacher-in-role as a drama-teaching strategy where she uses questioning
with 'the subtle tongue', hinting at the direction with phrases like 'I wonder
why . . .'. She saw the importance of proper teacher intervention to challenge and enable within the drama itself.

She is also renowned for her use of 'Mantle of the Expert', where children are given status and expertise by being put into the role of 'those
who know', for example as psychologists or architects. She recognizes the
validity of the knowledge and experience that the children bring with
them to the drama world.

Dorothy Heathcote identified the problem which is inherent in the usual
teacher/pupil relationship, teacher exploitation of power in a negative way
in the classroom, wittingly or unwittingly. Clearly the teacher is the one
who holds the power; this is important and that can never be fundamentally changed, nor should it be. However, the way that we as teachers
handle that position of power affects our teaching. We have to break
down our tendency to adopt the stereotype relationship and 'mind set'

NT: When the teacher's doing this and being Mum, do you think you ask questions more easily than asking questions of the teacher or is it the same?

BARRY: It's like a bit more harder when asking the Mum because you may know the teacher a lot more than you know the Mum.

I expected him to say it was easier asking Mum, but he sees Mum as a 'stranger', clearly fully accepting the fiction.

As I study the answers I begin to understand that, when the teacher in role is set up properly, it provokes more challenge and engagement *by creating a feeling of authenticity within the agreed fiction.*

Development of pupils' thinking and behaviour change

Steven, who began by saying 'no' to the idea of difference ends the interview with a remarkable metaphorical description of how he saw the role situation:

NT: Are the teachers generally behaving differently when they're in the drama from when they're teachers during the week?

STEVEN: It depends really. If they're just talking about what they're going to do, they're sort of like the same, but when they're actually acting, you don't really know it's a teacher really. You think it's someone coming into your classroom and the teachers are around the corner watching.

His expansive handling of the question shows that these are certainly his own ideas. Even 'it depends really' reveals that he is considering his response and not just trying to please the interviewer.

When she was shown the video, including Steven's definition, Sally Peters was astonished:

> He can actually see the difference when a teacher is a teacher – then they are giving instructions. ... That's really good that he sees it in that way because in the drama the teachers weren't round the corner at all. But almost when a teacher does go into role everything else does go out the window and here it's the role – he brings a whole new context to the classroom. 'We're not in the classroom, we're responding to this teacher in role.' He has very good understanding of the whole drama idea.

Because my study of the transcripts and the video revealed very important interactions involving Sally Peters and Steven, the main focus of this chapter is an examination of their perceptions of each other. The comments raise important general issues about the relationships between teachers and pupils.

I noticed on viewing the lesson that Steven seemed to be more confident when dealing with Sally's role of 'Mum' than with Sally as the teacher.

It is clear that Sally feels that she needs to keep an eye on Steven. Early in her interview she says, 'When I was teaching him I didn't feel he would give *unless I had him*. There were four lads there who could give me quite a lot of grief – Steven, Michael, Ivan and Lawrence'. Clearly a 'game' about discipline had developed in the week and she had to keep on top.

Just before going into role as Mum, Sally Peters, in role as the playschool supervisor, asked for ideas about what the supervisors should say to Thomas's mother.

> You've got Thomas's mum coming in. Thomas has just caused absolute chaos in our play scheme. We want to know what's going on. What sort of questions might you ask? [no pause] Steven?

There are many hands up and, as Sally admits, she asked him even though he didn't have his hand up. She did it in order to make sure she 'had him' rather than to really find out if he had a question. His response is:

STEVEN: (Sits upright. He pauses) Um – (Shuffles feet, wags hands up and down. Pause) Why did you ... er. (Pauses. Shrugs his shoulders as though he does not know what to say.)
SALLY: (Prompts) Why did ...?
STEVEN: (Struggles as though he was not going to say anything more.) Why did you ... (pause) ... be such a bully?

He fails to cope with this situation and gives an inappropriate contribution. Sally does not bother too much. She has achieved what she wanted and signalled the need for attention and closes the exchange with, 'We've got to ask questions to the Mum. Good ... Chris?'.

When she was shown the video of this Sally was able to see, 'He was very unsure – his body language' and she becomes much more understanding of what is happening to him ... 'I realise Steven had a lot to offer and I did focus on him'.

In contrast to his uncertainty above, when Mum is introduced to the supervisors, Steven is one of the first to volunteer information:

SALLY: Steven?
STEVEN: Are you aware of your son being disruptive and causing trouble in playschool?

On the video there is no stumbling or uncertainty in his delivery. He is confident and fluent. Sally picked this out:

She becomes very aware of how Steven is trapped by his behaviour and how her teacher response reinforces that feeling of failure:

> He's quite defensive – he's very aware ... he picked up on it with Teacher in Role. He can pick on intonation, facial expressions – he knew that my voice had changed and that was a sign from a positive attitude to angry.
>
> He knew that he'd done wrong – and he tried to justify me, to stick up for me.

How does the use of drama by the teacher enhance learning?

Finally, to draw the threads together I will quote Sally's conclusions about what is happening as she compares her experience of *being teacher* and *being in role* in the drama:

> They respond so much more to me in role – They are more likely to be honest in their opinion – more than they will be in real life – no come back. If I was doing something wrong they wouldn't be afraid to say so – no come back. Going back to this expected social situation, as a teacher, they're not going to question what I say.
>
> Teacher asks a question and they obviously have an idea in their head – the children – it clouds their actual answer to the question, is not thought about – 'I've got to get the answer right' or 'I've got to get the one the teacher wants to hear', rather than 'What's the answer to the question? What does it actually mean? What is my personal answer?'.
>
> The Teacher in Role gives the children the chance to say what they want – I think they're quite shocked by that. 'Ooh, I can actually say that.'
>
> The teacher works to guide them, stops them going off at a tangent, so they actually learn something ... but for actual ... what the children actually feel and say, the role gets more out of them.

From her own experience she draws a conclusion for me. She takes an example where she saw other trainees using role to teach science concepts:

> They used this professor to put across certain concepts and the children responded so well to the role – and the role played it down sort of like 'how can we do that bit?' and with the teacher sometimes the class are scared of that – because the teacher is always seen as knowing so much and gets everything right. – (And Steven is scared of getting things wrong and the other person is always right.)

If you give them the situation where it's 'I'm not really sure. What do you think?', they're forced to think about it so much more.

If they can see that the teacher is not this complete genius then they'll explore their own thoughts and ideas more.

It needs to be a balance in the classroom. It's not that the teacher can't put her ideas. Control and the whole authority thing is not to do with the teacher being at the front, children sitting down. It's just getting the balance between the teacher and the class, working together.

I have seen this deep involvement and attention with all age groups, including Reception and Nursery, where even young children respond to drama. Here are some example of roles a teacher might use in a drama constructed from traditional stories:

- a knave who has stolen tarts and now has to face the consequences;
- Goldilocks having to tell her father what she has done;
- a woman who has found a frightened Troll in her shed.

Suggestions for:

Further reading

Bolton, G., (1992) *New Perspectives on Classroom Drama*, London: Simon & Schuster Education.
  By a leading drama theorist, with some very useful examples to try.
Faulkner, D., Littleton, K., and Woodhead, M., (1998) *Learning Relationships in the Classroom*, London: Routledge.
  A key text for looking at how teachers relate to pupils.
Heathcote, D. and Bolton, G. (1995) *Drama for Learning, Dorothy Heathcote's Mantle of the Expert Approach to Education*, Portsmouth NH: Heinemann.
  One of the most important books on drama practice for classroom learning.
Kitson, N. and Spiby, I. (1997) *Drama 7–11: Developing Primary Teaching Skills*, London: Routledge.
  A practical and useful account of how to approach drama.
Neelands, J. (1992) *Learning Through Imagined Experience*, Cambridge: Cambridge University Press.
  This is excellent on the importance of drama for developing language.
Toye, N. and Prendiville, F. (2000) *Drama and Traditional Story for the Early Years*, London: Routledge.
  A very useful set of materials for using role with young children. One of the only texts devoted to that age group.
Woolland, B. (1993) *The Teaching of Drama in the Primary School*, London: Longman.

A key recent examination of theory, practice and very usable examples for all of the primary age range.

Further investigation

- Read a story and then negotiate taking a role of someone from the story whom the children can question for five minutes. See how they respond.
- Videotape an ordinary lesson and a lesson using role and analyse the pupils' responses. Interview some pupils about it.

Discussion with mentors in school

- Which pupils find it difficult to speak in class and why?
- Is it possible to use role and when and how would it be most effective?

Discussion on college-based courses

- Where does power reside in the classroom?
- What happens if trainees give clear signals that they do not know everything?
- What 'games' do you see being played between teacher and pupils? How much does 'guess what is in my head' occur?
- How do we get pupils to take responsibility for their own learning?

References

Cooper, P. and McIntyre, D. (1996) *Effective Classroom Learning: Teachers' and Pupils' Perspectives*, Milton Keynes: Open University Press.

Heathcote, D. (1998) 'Like Sisyphus, we keep pushing at the mountain', in T. Grady and C. O'Sullivan (eds) *A Head Taller: Developing a Humanising Curriculum Through Drama*, Birmingham: National Association for the Teaching of Drama.

Winston, J. (1998) *Drama, Narrative and Moral Education*, London: Falmer Press.

4 Student teachers in the infant classroom

Many hands make light work?

Suzanne Lea

> The learning child is not randomly discovering new ideas but is actively constructing new meanings under the carefully considered guidance of the practitioner.
>
> Edwards and Knight (1994:3)

Children learning

When I trained as an early-years teacher a moment of revelation came for me when I first heard of Piaget's theories of cognitive development. I had not previously realized that young children could have perspectives and ways of thinking which are different from those of adults. In fact I did not believe it! Then I became interested in the role of language in conceptual thinking, particularly the work of Vygotsky (1962, 1978). I began to realize how essential it is for teachers to understand that children learn by constructing meanings from their experiences, and that this can help us to understand the ways in which children try to make sense of the complex new social environment they encounter when they first start school.

All of us, in our attempts to make sense of new experience, do so by connecting the new events to familiar situations. The classic work of Margaret Donaldson (1978), which is also a helpful critique of Piaget's work, gives us insight into how we may help children make sense of their experience by creating familiar contexts for new challenges. A key question, therefore, is how can we make the school setting familiar so that young children can settle in painlessly?

Children leaving home for school

Most adults have fond or at least vivid memories of their earliest days at school. I remember my mother telling me that I would be at school for eleven years. I remember looking wistfully at the school gates thinking eleven years seemed a long time before I would see my mum again!

The transition from home to school can be traumatic for young children. Suddenly they have to become used to being one in a class of twenty or thirty. A whole set of bewildering rules and regulations must be recognized and learned. The transition from a secure and familiar environment to a busy, confusing school can be difficult. Reception class teachers are the key players in orchestrating this transition, ensuring that each child feels safe and 'at home'. Pollard (1985) agrees that the greatest threat to the child's ability to cope with the school situation is the way in which teachers implement the power aspect of their role. Children are often highly motivated by adult attention, not control. They want observers, listeners, approvers and commenters.

Getting to know parents and caregivers is an important part of these new beginnings. Home visits by the reception-class teacher and arranging visits to school prior to entry are common and effective. When I was Head of Infants we held afternoon and evening meetings for parents. The new children were invited to attend story sessions in the summer term. In order to ease the transition into school we had a staggered pattern of part-time admission for the first few weeks. We also provided information booklets so that parents and their children knew what to expect.

Infant teachers

Infant teachers play a vital role not only in ensuring the children make a good start on 'school work' but also in creating a comfortable and happy place, where each child learns how to make friends, to play alongside other children, and to fit into the social life of the school. Bennett's 1987 study found that a common statement by teachers on the aim for the first year at school was to help the child feel confident and secure and to help the child experience a sense of achievement.

One of the problems for Key Stage 1 teachers in 'handing over' their classes to student teachers is the very special nature of their relationship with 'their children'. Some teachers feel that their presence is essential to the children's feelings of security and are reluctant to risk 'unsettling' children who have made good progress.

However since children are used to a much more favourable adult/child ratio either at home or in nursery classes, the presence of one or more student teachers enables the children to have far greater individual attention than is normally possible.

The role of the student teacher

A key question of this inquiry is how children see student teachers fitting into their classroom. Further key influences upon my work as an educator and trainer of primary teachers were the social interactionist interpretations of classroom. This school of thought emphasizes classrooms as complex social settings within which each of the participants construct meanings according to their existing experience. A key notion from this perspective is the idea of 'the significant other' and the influential role that adults such as parents, guardians and teachers have in relation to young children. The classroom is seen as one of interaction where the participants learn as a result of their understanding of the situation.

The notion of the 'significant other' is particularly relevant when the role of the infant teacher is considered. Young children tend to think of their teacher as another mother or care-giver.

This then leads to the question: To what extent is a student teacher a 'significant other' in the eyes of the children? How can we find out the extent to which the child perceives the teacher and the student teacher as the same and therefore both as 'significant others'?

Methodology

The focus of my inquiry was to identify young children's perceptions of their student teachers and any differences between pupils' perceptions of their class teacher and of the student teacher. St Martin's College has a policy of introducing students as 'teachers' when they are on teaching practice. The student teachers were in their second year of a four-year BA QTS course. The three schools in my study had different types of catchment areas and different types of Reception class organization. The inquiry took place towards the latter part of the students' five-week block teaching placement. I was known in the schools because of my work as a college tutor. The ten students involved were all working with Reception and Key Stage 1 children and I talked to children from each of the ten classes.

Key questions

- What are the perceptions of young children about their student teachers?
- Are these perceptions different from the children's perceptions about their class teachers?
- Are there differences in perception between Reception children who have just made the transition to school and older Key Stage 1 children?
- How might I uncover the perceptions of these very young children?
- What would be an appropriate way of gathering data when the children did not know me?

Children's drawings

There is a tradition of using children's drawings to obtain data. It is an appropriate approach, particularly for young children, since they are just beginning to combine experience and language. Drawings enable the researcher to access children's ideas which they are perhaps too young to express verbally.

Buckham (1994) states that drawing is a natural system that young children adopt to symbolize objects and events. Since children do a lot of drawing as part of their school work I decided to ask the children to draw a picture of their student and class teachers.

The pilot study

The pilot study was carried out with children from two classes in the same school. One of the key questions at this time was what would be the best way to work with children whom I did not know. I also wanted to try out ways of wording my questions and instructions.

One of the problems of asking children to draw is that they tend to draw imaginary scenes rather than things that have really happened. Leanne drew herself and her teacher flying kites in the park, although this had never happened! (Figure 4.1). Kieran drew his class teacher helping him learn how to skip, although again the teacher had not done this.

Whilst these were 'imaginary' events, the pictures could be interpreted as revealing the child's perception of the teacher as a person who plays with them, rather than in the more formal teaching role.

I decided to ask the children to draw a specific picture relating to the student and the class teacher. I asked the children about their drawings

Figure 4.1 Leanne drew herself and her teacher flying kites in the park, although this had never happened

and encouraged them to talk about what they were drawing. It is not so much the pictures themselves that are useful as the combination of drawing and description. The drawing makes the thoughts and feelings of the children accessible both to themselves and to the researcher. Since I was interested in the affective nature of the role of the infant teacher I decided to ask the children to draw a picture of their class and student teachers 'looking after them'. The children tended to interpret 'looking after' quite literally! They drew a student teacher putting a plaster on a knee or picking them up when they had fallen.

A further consideration was the choosing of the children and how many I could work with at any one time. I left the selection to the class teacher. Children were selected who were likely to be confident enough to speak to someone they did not know. In the pilot study I had decided on a group of four but this was too many for extended talk – and the children tended to copy each other! I decided to talk to two children at a time.

The study

I used as a guiding principle, that it is only close observation of the drawing activity itself and the talk that accompanies it that reveal the range of the child's thinking. I asked the children to draw a picture of their student and their class-teacher. I encouraged them to talk about their drawing whilst asking them about how their teachers look after them.

Figure 4.2 'A student teacher putting a plaster on a knee'. Children interpreted 'looking after' quite literally

The children did recognize the care-giving role of their teachers. One child depicted both the student teacher and the class teacher with hearts on their clothes.

Figures 4.3 and *4.4* Children recognized the care-giving role of their teachers. The student and the teacher both have hearts on their clothes

However, although Year 2 children attempted to describe the care-giving role of the teacher they found it difficult to articulate their ideas.

SL: How does Miss Morris (student teacher) look after you?
MARY: Nice.
SL: What do you mean ... nice?
MARY: Kind.
JOANNE: She's nice to us.

However, from the children's drawings and their accompanying talk there appear to be two quite distinctive aspects of the children's perceptions of both their class and student teachers which appeared to be more signifi- cant to the children than their perception of the role of their teacher as

Figure 4.5 Children drew pictures of themselves engaged in literacy and numeracy activities

a care-giver. The children drew pictures of 'school' events, showing themselves engaged in activities related to literacy or numeracy. They often
depicted specific features of the lesson such as the resources used.

Sarra is a Year 1 child:

SL: What is Miss Saunders (student teacher) doing?
SARRA: She is holding up the cards.
SL: What cards?
SARRA: Two and ten.

Here the children indicated few differences in perception between their
view of the class teacher and their view of the student teacher.

Martin and Kevin are Year 2 children:

SL: How is Mrs Phillips (class-teacher) looking after you?
MARTIN: Er ... looking at your work. ...

Figure 4.6 Drawings often showed key features of a lesson and the resources used

KEVIN: Mrs Phillips is wearing a pretty dress today.
SL: What is Mrs Phillips doing to look after you?
KEVIN: She is learning us things.
She is doing the same things as Miss Roberts (student teacher).
She is looking after us and learning us new words . . .
they both really do the same things.

Cathie is a five-year-old Reception child:

CATHIE: (talking about her picture) That's me and that's Miss Godwin
(student teacher).
SL: What were you doing?
CATHIE: You have to write a sentence down and I got stuck.
SL: What did you get stuck on?
CATHIE: My word of school.

Two of the children drew their class teachers playing games with them
such as skipping and playing with the cars. There were no children's drawings of student teachers engaged in play activities.

The second key feature of the drawings was the children's perception
of who their teacher was in relation to the organization of their classes.
Reception children know they are school pupils and that all the adults in
the classroom and school are their school teachers. The class teacher, the
student teacher, the teacher from the class next door, the work experience student who had only been in school two weeks – all were identified
as 'their' teachers.

In contrast the Year 2 children had a very clear idea of the organization of the school and the consequent role of their teachers. Two Year 2
girls talked about the assignments of children into ability sets for literacy
and numeracy lessons.

SL: What does Miss Morris do when she helps you?
GILL: I don't know what she does . . . I can't remember . . . I know what
she does . . . the board. . . . Are you doing the board?
JOE: No.
GILL: I couldn't remember because I'm a new circle. I used to be in that
area
JOE: . . . and I'm an old circle.
SL: How many teachers have you?
JOE: Just two in our classroom.
JOE: . . . and there are other teachers in there (pointing to the adjoining
area) and in the other years but we don't know them especially the
headteacher.
GILL: I'm here for numeracy and number.
SL: . . . what does Miss Morris do with you?

GILL: Poetry . . . that's all . . . I'm drawing her earrings and her brooch and her glasses . . . sitting in a chair. . . . A table where we have our big bookstand. . . . I'm going to look what the big book is called. . . .

They drew details of specific lessons. Often a key feature was the way in which the lesson was organized. Children depicted themselves sitting on the carpet for shared book experiences and sitting at tables for numeracy work.

Other features of the literacy hour were identified by younger children who drew signs the teacher placed on the table for the different groups.

Danny aged five:

DANNY: My teacher (class teacher) is Mrs Brown and she's over there! She helps you if you've got hard work.
I can read anything.
I can read signs . . . they say. . . .
I am working with the teacher.
I am working alone.

Figure 4.7 One child depicted the student teacher using praise

A further feature of children's perceptions was the children's knowledge of classroom rules and discipline. Children were aware of the role of the student teacher and class teacher in terms of discipline, even when the 'telling off' was directed at another child. One child also depicted the student teacher using praise.

Within the notion of discipline the children demonstrated that they were aware of the rules of the classroom. Some of the children drew themselves with their hands up waiting to answer a question.

Jason is a Year 1 child:

SL: What is Miss Saunders doing in your picture?
JASON: She is holding it up for us to see the picture.
SL: Which book is it?
JASON: A Toy Story book.
   That's me with my hand up.
SL: Why have you got your hand up?
JASON: She has asked us something about the book.

One very able Year 1 pupil had a clear notion of the reciprocal nature of questions in the classroom. She used speech bubbles to show herself and the teacher asking questions.

SL: What are you doing (in the picture)?
BARBARA: I'm drawing me and Lisa putting our hands up.
SL: Why are you putting your hands up?
BARBARA: Because we're wanting to ask different questions.

The key features of the perceptions of this sample of children appeared to be notions of the organization of the school and the interaction between themselves and their teachers within this framework. Children tended to depict the task-orientated nature of the classroom, particularly in relation to literacy and numeracy, although two children's drawings showed their class teachers engaging in play activities with them.

Conclusion

There appears to be some evidence that the Reception children did perceive the teacher's role differently from the Year 2 children. This was not because they saw their relationship with the teacher as different but because the children became increasingly aware of the teacher's role in organizing the classroom and planning particular kinds of learning activities. As children become more accustomed to different grouping arrangements they begin to have a clear idea of the organizational framework of their school and the role of both themselves and the teachers within it. Classrooms were shown as very much task orientated, particularly by the older children. Here often the role of the teacher and student teacher was referred to as being 'they help me to learn'. Children in Reception classes do not seem to have such a task-orientated perception. They put greater emphasis upon play, even when this is imaginary.

None of the young children viewed student teachers as different from their class teachers in terms of role. However, when I asked who their teacher was, the children always mentioned their class teacher first. The children understood the classroom rules, such as putting their hands up, but had no explanation for the reasons for the rules.

Young children enter school with a whole range of understandings of the world. Talking to these children about their drawings gave some insights into the ways in which, as they progress from Reception to Year 2, children construct for themselves an understanding of the purposes of school and the special activities that take place in school, the ways in which children and classes are organized, and the multi-faceted roles of teachers. These children seemed to make no distinction between the roles of their class teachers and student teachers.

Suggestions for:

Further investigations

- Ask the children to draw a picture of their teacher (with the teacher's permission), and a picture of you in school.
- What episode of classroom life does each drawing represent? What does this tell you about how the children perceive the teacher's role; your role?

Discussion with mentors in school

- Find out the school approach to transition from home/nursery for children starting school. How does the school provide for continuity?

Discussion on college-based courses

- Identify the forms of organization from your school placement for the teaching of literacy and numeracy; how did the children learn to understand these?

References

Bennett, N. (1987) *The Aims of Teachers and Parents for Children in their First Year at School*, Windsor: NFER.

Buckham, J. (1994) 'Teachers' understanding of children's drawing', in C. Aubrey (ed.) *The Role of Subject Knowledge in the Early Years of Schooling*, London: Falmer Press.

Donaldson, M. (1978) *Children's Minds*, London: Fontana.

Edwards, A. and Knight, P. (1994) *Effective Early Years Education – Teaching Young Children*, Buckingham: Open University Press.

Pollard, A. (1985) *The Social World of the Primary School*, London: Holt Rinehart and Winston.

Sharp, C. and Turner, G. (1987) *Four Year Olds in School*, Windsor: NFER.

Vygotsky, L.S. (1962) *Thought and Language*, New York: Riley.

Vygotsky, L.S. (1978) *Mind in Society*, London: Harvard University Press.

Part III

Do pupils learn what trainee teachers teach?

5　Geography

Can't you tell us the answer Miss?

Neil Simco

The process of learning to teach is slow, complex and demanding. Both personal and professional development run in parallel. Teachers need to understand how classrooms work and to see that their influence is central; to acknowledge that a decision taken at one moment for one child may have multiple and far-reaching consequences for everyone. Teachers need to have a wide range of techniques and professional skills such as how to plan lessons, to assess children, to manage time and to relate to parents, school staff and governors. How do children learn? What is 'effective' teaching? How do government policies influence what goes on in the classroom. Beyond all this and much more, each of us needs to develop and articulate a personal philosophy of teaching. This is a formidable professional requirement and one that is frequently underestimated by tutors and mentors.

When I first became a teacher educator, I quickly realized that learning to teach effectively is difficult. However at that time I was unable to explain in detail *how* it was demanding. In my own specialist subject, I knew that trainees were able to state clearly their own theories of how geography is best taught, but I also knew that even the most capable found it difficult to put their theories into practice in the classroom. One student whom I remember, David Alsop, believed that children must be given ownership of the definitions, content and process when studying an unknown region. This would enable pupils to 'get inside' the fabric of that place as opposed to merely developing 'cold' factual knowledge. Yet my classroom observations suggested that David used approaches which meant that he defined the direction of the study and that the outcome was almost pre-determined. The children knew specific facts about the Kenyan village under study but did not understand the issues and dilemmas faced by the villagers. This raised a series of questions: Why did David find it difficult to incorporate his beliefs about teaching into his actual classroom work? What did the children make of his teaching? Did they understand anything of his beliefs? What key messages did they receive about the nature of geography?

As I set about exploring these questions the work of Lee Shulman became a useful point of departure. Shulman (1986) devised a key concept which he called 'pedagogical content knowledge'; knowledge that 'goes beyond knowledge of subject matter alone to the dimension of subject matter for teaching. I still speak of content knowledge here, but of the particular form of content knowledge that embodies aspects of content most germaine to its teachability' (p. 10). In other words, the act of teaching demands a particular kind of subject knowledge that is related to knowing how to teach that subject. To develop this kind of pedagogical content knowledge is arguably far from straightforward and yet it is essential if children are to encounter experiences and undertake activities which reflect their teacher's beliefs about the subject in question. Several researchers have explored this notion of pedagogical content knowledge further. Most recently Rosie Turner-Bisset (1999) makes a distinction between pedagogical content knowledge – 'beliefs about the subject' – and 'general educational beliefs'. This gives us a further helpful insight into why the translation of subject beliefs into practical teaching is difficult. There are two dimensions, one related to the specific subject and one to the curriculum as a whole.

Given the importance of Shulman's work in furthering my own understanding of how we learn to teach, it is not surprising that he came to mind when I undertook the fieldwork in preparation for this chapter. This involved a number of recorded conversations with Charlotte Simms, a primary geography specialist student on a BA (QTS) course. Charlotte was nearing the end of her Final Block Placement at the time of the investigation. I had been her tutor for nearly four years and I had become familiar with her views and beliefs about geography. By the final stage of the course she was able to talk about these beliefs in considerable depth and detail; indeed this course was designed to encourage the students to discuss and refine their beliefs. Given all this clarity and certainty, I was interested in finding out whether the children Charlotte was teaching had any sense of her oft-stated views about effective teaching. What did the children think that Charlotte's geography teaching was all about?

It was these kinds of consideration which led me to devise the key question for the case study: 'To what extent are Charlotte's personal beliefs about effective geography teaching apparent in her teaching such that children have an understanding of the "kind" of geography that is being taught?' I wanted to find out more about the Shulman notion of pedagogical content knowledge in practice. I had a hunch that the children would not see Charlotte's teaching in the same way that she saw it and if so I wanted to analyse why this was the case.

Before her placement began I interviewed Charlotte about her plans for teaching geography. Her work was to centre around a local study concerning a by-pass to the village of Totterham where the school was located, and I wanted to find out how Charlotte's beliefs were reflected in her planning. Our first focus was on whether she considered the children should have ownership over inquiry or whether it would be teacher-directed. I also asked Charlotte whether she believed that the actual processes involved in children's geographical inquiry were more important than the end products – in other words, whether the 'taking part' was more beneficial to children's learning than the final product. A final focus related to the extent to which co-operation and collaboration would be emphasized in the class. I also collected copies of her medium-term plans, lesson plans, classroom resources and eventually the children's work. If I was to see whether the children realized that Charlotte's teaching reflected a certain set of beliefs I needed to be clear about the nature of her beliefs. Once the placement had started, I observed the children at work, and interviewed them, focusing on the extent to which they had some understanding of Charlotte's beliefs.

Charlotte specified three key elements in her plan for geography work over nine weeks: skills work on imaging and mental mapping, the real by-pass inquiry, and a fictional by-pass inquiry.

Imaging and mental mapping were taught first to provide a context for the actual study of the by-pass. There were two major aims: 'Children will understand the term personal map' and 'Children will understand that personal maps are unique'. Children began by drawing a map of an imaginary journey. They went on to draw different kinds of maps to generate discussion about what the 'formal' common characteristics of maps are. A series of activities then focused on these characteristics, particularly scale, key, symbol and grid. So that: 'Children will be able to draw a scale map of the classroom' and 'Children will understand how to use a key and symbols on a 1 : 50,000 OS map'. The section on co-ordinates involved such activities as asking children to place certain symbols on a map of an imaginary island. The final part of the skills section was more directly linked to the by-pass inquiry – the notion of thematic maps. Charlotte then began the intensive work on the proposed by-pass, for which she had allowed one week. There were three main lessons. In the first lesson, the children were divided into groups representing the major stakeholders: residents, environmentalists and landowners. Each group used a blank outline map of Totterham and information on financial and environmental costs (Figure 5.1) to decide on a route and to justify their plan to the other groups.

Charlotte's aim for the second lesson was that 'Children will be able to identify that there are many different views concerning the by-pass'. Her intention was to create a context for children to debate a key decision based on their acquired geographical knowledge. During the final lesson, the children participated in role at a town meeting to decide the route of the Totterham by-pass. Each group stated its beliefs about the by-pass route, questions were tabled and then a vote was taken. Charlotte wanted the children to understand the idea of consensus – that the view which they eventually supported might not be the one they originally favoured.

Costs to Consider

The by-pass will cost £2 million per km.

A bridge will cost £10 million.

Building a junction or crossing another road will cost £1/2 million.

If your route passes within 100m (1cm on the map) of a building you will have to pay compensation of £250,000.

You also have £1 million to spend on landscaping (including tree planting to reduce noise).

Which route is cheapest . . . financially? Best for residents? Environmentally?

Figure 5.1 Information provided for the children about the Totterham Inquiry

To find out more about the match between Charlotte's beliefs and the children's views of the geography work, I interviewed Emily, Ashley and Katy. The interviews revealed a number of interesting issues in how the class saw Charlotte's teaching; some provided remarkably clear insights into the success which Charlotte had in conveying her beliefs about geography teaching and learning. All three children understood that Charlotte believed in the importance of the children themselves finding out information.

NS: When you do geography with Miss Simms what do you do if you need some information about the by-pass?
EMILY: Miss Simms explains it in a different way.
ASHLEY: With Miss Simms you have to work it out yourself. She asks you to do the work more and find out information.
KATY: Yes, Miss Simms asks what different words mean. You have to find out what activist means. You have to do something about it – by yourself – when you want to find something out.

The children clearly did not expect Miss Simms to hand out factual information. Charlotte has created a classroom context where the children are expected to a certain extent to be independent. I went back to the transcript of my earlier conversations with Charlotte to see if she had expressed these kinds of beliefs. She had stated that if children are undertaking a geographical inquiry there needs to be a progression from inquiry which is defined by the teacher to one where children have more ownership over their own learning. The following excerpt illustrates this and indeed was closely reflected in her planning which provided opportunities for the children to acquire geographical skills before they embarked on the actual inquiry.

CHARLOTTE: At the beginning of the year, particularly, there is a need to give a basis and then let them take ownership. . . . If the school encourages inquiry you could give them [the children] less to start with.

A comparison between this excerpt and the interviews with Ashley, Emily and Katy reveals that Charlotte's beliefs and the children's interpretation of Charlotte's teaching correspond. The children clearly understand that they must find out information for themselves and use it to develop an argument for their by-pass choice. This was particularly evident during the final lesson when each group had to make reference to their work to support their choice for the by-pass route. Emily was in the 'landowners' group and rigorously defended her view that the road should be built on the other side of the village to her own land on the grounds of cost! It was very apparent to me that Emily had enjoyed taking a central part in the role play.

There is evidence that Charlotte believed children should have some ownership over their inquiry, and that her approach to teaching enabled this to occur to the extent that the children were explicitly aware of this. However, in other areas Charlotte was less successful in translating her beliefs into her teaching.

If you are aiming to develop skills of enquiry then process is important. This applies in this particular local study. Generally process is more important – it's the children's own thinking. I would put process above product. Children will already *know* about their area and that knowledge bit is important. They are required to learn about the place they're in. It's not most important. They need to know how to find out new things rather than just being told. . . . In an inquiry children need to discuss their ideas so they can refine their ideas between them. I encourage this as much as possible. Sharing ideas and working together is important . . . I would see this as more important than a lone study – although this is also relevant sometimes.

The children's views indicated that Charlotte had not been successful in implementing these beliefs:

NS: What did you find out when you did this work [the local study]?
EMILY: We learned what a co-ordinate was and how to put this in the right place.
KATY: I learned what a by-pass is and I learned some new words.

NS: Can you tell me some of these?

KATY: One is activist and this is like an eco-warrior which means someone who fights for the environment.

Emily and Katy were most clear about having acquired some factual information rather than the process-related elements of learning which were central to Charlotte's beliefs. When I explored this idea further it was clear that Emily and Katy in particular did not see that part of Charlotte's agenda was to have the children discuss and refine ideas. For them, the part of the project where they worked alone to 'find out facts' was the heart of the inquiry. Emily was unclear about *why* the class was studying possible routes for the by-pass. She said that the point of investigating possible routes was for different groups to find the cheapest option, or the 'best for the environment' or the 'best for the residents', but they were 'just doing it in the class'. She did not see the work as connected to the actual by-pass proposal for her town.

I mentioned that alongside the actual Totterham by-pass study the children worked on a fictional by-pass scheme during a Literacy Hour. The fictional by-pass curriculum materials included newspaper reports, letters to the Council, official documents and so forth. I asked the children to compare the relative difficulty of investigating the fictional and the real by-pass.

ASHLEY: It was easier to do the other by-pass work [using the published curriculum materials] because there was more information. I didn't have enough information about the Totterham by-pass. I wanted to find out more.

NS: What do you mean?

ASHLEY: It would be good to go out of school and look at where they wanted the by-pass to be. I'd like to draw a sketch ... or talk to some people about what they think.

Ashley's comments focus on the lack of information in the real by-pass work. Use of photographs, site visits to different aspects of the proposed by-pass routes and interviews with local people must have given the children further insight into the importance of the processes of inquiry in geography.

I concluded that whilst the children appeared to understand that Charlotte believed children should have some ownership over their own learning, they were less clear about other areas of her beliefs. Their image of Charlotte's teaching was fundamentally different to her own. She had a strongly expressed view about the importance of collaboration, whereas Emily and Katy considered factual information to be important. Ashley was unsure about the process of investigation because he did not have enough information to help him make an informed decision about the by-pass.

I want to return now to some of the statements which I made earlier in the chapter. I suggested that the process of learning to teach is slow, complex and demanding, and that, in particular, I feel that whilst many students are clear about their beliefs and values about teaching a subject, they find it difficult to translate these beliefs into practice. This relates to Shulman's notion of pedagogical content knowledge, essentially the knowledge that is required to translate subject knowledge into effective teaching. The case study suggests that Charlotte found some difficulty in translating her beliefs about geography teaching into a reality that was apparent to the children.

At this early stage in her teaching experience Charlotte had limited pedagogical content knowledge although I would argue that this is no indictment of her teaching. She is a successful student who is clear about her philosophy of geography teaching, is able to establish and maintain effective working relationships with the children and is committed to the whole process of learning to teach.

Why then were the children unable in some instances to see Charlotte's beliefs reflected in her teaching? I suggest that a speculative answer may be found in an exploration of the origins of the beliefs which children and teachers bring to the classroom. Charlotte had a clear philosophy of effective teaching and learning in geography. The children's past experience of geography work will have influenced how they perceived Charlotte's teaching. In taking these views further, I need to refer to the literature on classroom social processes. Here, the work of Andrew Pollard is particularly useful. In a 1985 study, he looked at the main 'classroom actors' and suggested that both teachers and children come to that classroom with understandings and preconceptions. He suggests that children's views of the classroom are determined by two factors. He terms the first of these 'role factors'. These are the children's understanding of their role in the classroom in terms of, for example, how they are to behave, the extent of their responsibility for their own learning, and acceptable protocol when addressing each other and their teachers. The second is 'biographical factors'. These concern the influence of their personal history inside and outside school. These two factors may be linked by using Doyle's (1986) emphasis on the notion of the history of the class as an important social consideration. The shared class history is part of each child's personal biography and is a determinant of how children construct their roles. In Charlotte's class the children's previous experience of geography teaching offered a different set of beliefs than those promoted by Charlotte. Mr Philips, the class teacher, had a more formal style with more emphasis on knowledge and skills than empathy and process. It seemed to me that Emily and Katy were aware that Charlotte's beliefs were different from Mr Philips, but were unsure how they were different.

Pedagogical content knowledge is shaped by a richly developed classroom context where children's existing understandings are real and need to be fully understood before new teachers can begin to change it by introducing their own beliefs and values. It may have been that the children's partial understanding of Charlotte's beliefs can be explained by her underestimation of the need both to make these beliefs explicit and to know and understand the beliefs which the children already held.

Teachers as well as children have perceptions and backgrounds which influence their understanding of teaching and learning. Student teachers are themselves still learners within the process of formal education and inevitably have strong views on teacher roles and the complex experience of being taught. I suggest that there is another factor which is increasingly influential. This is the influence of national policy initiatives (such as the QCA Curriculum Review published in September 1999).

For Charlotte the geography specialist course had been a particularly important part of her biography. In each area of the course there were opportunities for student teachers to make explicit their beliefs about teaching approaches. Work in a local school on a new shopping development and the use of vacant shop was used as a context for a wider discussion about ownership and audience in actual local studies. Who owns the work and who is it for? A variety of approaches including role play and photography were chosen by trainees when teaching about a distant place. Each teaching session was analysed and discussed. The course assessment required Charlotte to write a detailed analysis of her own beliefs about the subject. As a course tutor I felt assured that Charlotte knew what she believed, but perhaps like Charlotte in her classroom, I underestimated the influence of other biographical factors, particularly her own experiences as a pupil. Here, much research has pointed to the prevalence of pre-training concepts held by student teachers in the process of learning to teach (for example Calderhead and Robson 1991). Students' pre-training experiences and general life history will be particularly important in influencing the development of beliefs about effective teaching during the period of training. As Kagan (1992: 154) states, 'the personal beliefs and images that pre-service candidates bring to the process of teacher education usually remain inflexible'.

This same perspective has been cited by James Calderhead and Susan Shorrock (1997: 187). They consider the place of professional learning concerned with the 'processes of assimilation': the relationship between students' beliefs and values and their teaching. This relationship is problematic. Reporting on their research (1997: 168) they mention that 'even though the students might have a more elaborate perception of their situation ... they frequently still lacked the appropriate knowledge to deal with it'. This is particularly so as students are required to express their beliefs in at least two stages – initial planning and then the actual teaching situation. In planning and in teaching it is possible for beliefs to be mediated and changed due to the lack of pedagogical content knowledge.

Pollard's analysis of the context of classroom participants helps us to understand why pedagogical content knowledge is difficult to acquire and apply (Pollard, 1995). It demands that you know what you believe, that you are able to translate this into planning for children's learning, that you understand how to put this planning into practice, that you understand the children's biographies and beliefs, and that you can spot significant moments when a key question or intervention can change a child's views of the subject. In this way the idea of pedagogical content knowledge is seen as problematic. The reality of a complex classroom environment to which all the participants bring their own understandings and preconceptions about roles and the process of learning does indeed make learning to teach complex, slow and demanding. To be clear about beliefs related to effective teaching and learning in a subject is difficult enough. To be able to apply this moment by moment in the reality of the classroom is an on-going challenge.

Suggestions for:

Further reading

Shulman, L. (1986) 'Those who understand: knowledge and growth in teaching', *Educational Researcher* 15(2) 4–14.
Turner-Bisset, R. (1999) 'The knowledge base of the expert teacher', *British Educational Research Journal* 25(1) 39–56.

Further investigations

How do children perceive what they have learned? Explore children's perceptions about what they see as important in their learning through using a range of techniques such as:

- semi-structured interviews with individual and groups of children before and after a unit of work to probe their understanding about areas of learning which are seen as of most value;
- encouraging children to write evaluations of their work, focusing on what they've learned;
- working with children in a small group situation to record a group consensus of what has been learned.

Discussion with mentors in school

- What key messages are you giving children about the importance you attach to various areas of their learning? (For example if you consider that the process of enquiry in a geographical investigation is important, does this come through in your teaching?)

- Does your approach to teaching geography really convey the beliefs you have about the subject? (Or are you inadvertently giving children different messages about what you believe to be important?)

Discussion on college-based courses

- What are your beliefs about effective teaching in geography? Using a response partner write a paragraph which summarizes these. Hold this up to scrutiny with other student colleagues.
- Do your beliefs change over time?
- What factors influence any changes which may occur?

References

Calderhead, J. and Robson, M. (1991) 'Images of teaching: student teachers' early conceptions of classroom practice', *Teaching and Teacher Education* 7(1): 1–8.

Calderhead, J. and Shorrock, S.B. (1997) *Understanding Teacher Education*, London: Falmer Press.

Doyle, W. (1986) 'Classroom organisation and management', in M.C. Wittrock (ed.) *Handbook of Research on Teaching*, New York: Macmillan.

Kagan, D. (1992) 'Professional growth amongst pre-service and beginning teachers', *Review of Educational Research* 62(2): 129–169.

Pollard, A. (1985) *The Social World of the Primary School*, London: Cassell.

Shulman, L. (1986) 'Those who understand: knowledge growth in teaching', *Educational Researcher* 15(2): 4–14.

Turner-Bisset, R. (1999) 'The knowledge bases of the expert teacher', *British Educational Research Journal* 25(1): 39–56.

6 The properties that matter

Children's perceptions of student teachers in science

Anne Riggs and Aftab Gujral

'Science is brilliant'

Samantha, a Year 4 pupil, was commenting on learning science with a student teacher. All of the forty children interviewed in February and March 1999 agreed. And while it is good to know that children have such a positive opinion about doing science, we wanted to discover what they were learning.

Interviews with the children

Twenty-two of the children were in Year 6 and eighteen children in Year 4, in six primary schools. They had been taught by seven student teachers who had finished a second-year block school experience two weeks before the interviews. We talked to the children informally in groups of four to six (forty interviews in all). We had established a protocol of four set questions with the children able to take as much time as they wanted to answer. Additional questions were asked to clarify and probe the responses the children gave. Interviews were audio-recorded and transcribed. The questions, asked in no particular order, were:

- Do you like science?
- What did you do in science with Miss/Mr X (the student teacher)?
- Is there any difference in the science you did with Miss/Mr X and the science you do with Miss/Mr Y (the class teacher)?
- Do you make guesses about what will happen?

Both of us analysed the transcripts independently. We decided to arrange the children's comments in five categories: practical work is enjoyable; making predictions; fair testing; writing; and using computers.

Practical work is enjoyable

Comments from Year 6 pupils included:

> Doing an experiment makes us feel important.
> When you are doing experiments, you learn more than when you are just reading about it.
> Everyone likes it because it's experiments, not just bookwork.
> Good doing experiments; boring when they didn't work.
> We learned to work with each other in different groups.

The children found that working with student teachers was enjoyable because they were enthusiastic, arranged a lot of practical work, were approachable when things went wrong, brought in their own resources and encouraged the pupils to bring in resources. A Year 4 pupil explained 'I liked playing with his [friend's] magnets'.

Student teachers encouraged pupils to try out experiments at home. In one Year 6 class the children were enthusiastic about the homework that had been set the previous week. 'We had to find out which substances were acids and which were alkaline.'

Making predictions

In the Programmes of Study of the 1995 National Curriculum Science Order, children are required to: Ask questions such as 'How?' 'Why?' 'What will happen if . . .?'. They need to learn 'that making predictions can be useful when planning what to do'. We did not use the word 'prediction' in our questions but instead asked the children whether they had to guess what would happen or say what they think would happen in science classes. This was a familiar idea, but we wanted to find out what the children thought prediction involved when para-phrased as 'guessing what would happen'. A Year 6 pupil replied:

> Guessing is saying what you think will happen. We made parachutes and tied toys on them. One parachute had a tear in the side. We had to guess which toy would land first. I thought the one with the hole in it would. People die if their parachute has a hole in it.

A Year 4 pupil who was investigating sugars of different types, said:

> We had to say which would dissolve best.

A Year 6 pupil who was carrying out an investigation of the strength of different types of paper as part of the unit on Materials, commented:

I thought the brown paper would be the strongest. I guessed this because people use brown paper to wrap parcels.

All the children understood the process of predicting, and sometimes drew on their everyday knowledge and experience. Producing possible explanations or hypotheses, which can be tested is an essential process in science. This prediction, this 'possible explanation', must be tested.

The children were able to show that the brown paper was the strongest by using different types of paper to support the same weight and to measure the tearing point of each. Children need to develop the ability to make predictions that are linked to practical investigations. Planning the test procedure is important. Part of such planning is 'fair testing'.

We asked a group of Year 6 children whether they made guesses or predictions in any other subjects. Peter said that they did in mathematics but this was actually more like estimating and the rest of his group agreed. That the guessing in mathematics is estimating was also put forward by another group of Year 6 children. One said:

In maths we say how long we think the table is and then we measure it.

Another child offered an example of prediction:

In science after we say what we think will happen we do experiments.

When we asked the children why they thought making and testing predictions was part of science, none offered an answer. Further probing did not lead to any suggestions. Asked if they thought 'real' scientists made guesses about what would happen and then carried out experiments, the children knew that scientists carried out experiments, but the suggestion that scientists make predictions before carrying out experiments was a completely new idea to the children. Linking school science to the work of research scientists is an important concept – it leads to an understanding of what science is and how it differs from the inquiry process in other subjects.

It is actually very difficult to produce a definition of what science is; something that has long been recognized. What we can say is, science is what scientists do. Scientists produce theories by carrying out observations and experiments to try to establish their ideas. Wynne Harlen, who has done much to forward primary science, translates some of what scientists do in this way:

It is important to realize that ... there are some activities involving process skills, attitudes and concepts that are specifically scientific and are especially significant for that reason. The process skills are those relating to the testing of hypotheses (possible explanations) by experiment (fair testing).

(Harlen, 1985: 6)

Practical work is important in primary-school science, though of course books, web-sites and CD ROMs also have a place in science teaching. There is perhaps a temptation to restrict work to the 'new technology', but this must not be the only experience children have for testing their ideas. The interview findings indicate that children can feel 'short-changed' when they have to use non-practical investigative methods.

Sue, a Year 6 pupil, said:

> We make guesses and then find out by looking in books. It is much better with Miss Godwin, we make things and measure what happens.

And one of her fellow pupils, Ben, added that:

> We learn more than when we just read about it.

Not all the children, however, liked doing practical work: four girls said they wanted to be told. Why they said this was not explored, but possible reasons could be lack of confidence or understanding, inexperience of working on one's own or in groups and unfamiliarity with practical work. This latter reason is possible given that all the children said they did more practical work with students than with their class teachers.

Fair testing in practical work

Fair testing is concerned with exploring relationships between variables or factors. The 1995 Key Stage 2 programme of study (DFE, 1995) describes this as changing one factor and observing and or measuring the effect (other factors are kept the same).

All the children interviewed were familiar with fair testing and they were able to explain and give examples of fair testing they had done.

A Year 6 pupil provided a description:

> We had some sugar, some salt and some sand and we had to find out which one dissolved best. We put the salt, sugar and sand in water. The same amount had to be put in the same amount of water. We stirred all the pots for the same time and as near as we could to each other and measured how long it took for the bits to disappear.

Another pupil added:

> We measured the temperature of the water. It had to be the same.

Asked why, the children replied that the salt and sugar disappeared better in hot water. One child said this was 'like sugar dissolving in a cup of tea'. The children understood the need to keep all the factors the same except the one they were measuring – time. The comment about the cup of tea indicates not only that the child understood the investigative process but also was able to identify the variables to be considered. Qualter (1996: 36) discusses the need to see 'the reasons for the fair test' ... to know why 'fairness is important in [an] experiment and what the fairness should involve'. In order to do this children must make links between process and concepts. The children working with parachutes understood the need to use the same area of material and to drop the parachutes from the same height, and they also used conceptual understanding about gravity and air resistance.

Recording and reporting

Children enjoyed the practical experiences, making predictions and testing them but the predominant factor they did not enjoy was writing about them. Asked what they liked best about science, two girls in Year 4 said writing, but this was not typical. A group of Year 4 children said writing up science was boring: the student teacher who had worked with the first group had required the pupils to copy what she had written on the board. A group of Year 6 children agreed. Five of the seven student teachers appeared to have a set format for writing about practical work: the children actually said for 'writing up experiments'. The format was:

What we thought would happen.
A drawing of what we used.
What happened. / What it looked like.

This format is similar to the report writing required in many secondary school science classes:

Title – Experiment to find out ...
Apparatus
Method
Results
Conclusion

That the majority of the children interviewed found writing boring is reminiscent of the findings from a research project about student teachers' perceptions of science and science education (Riggs and Hayhurst, 1995). Asked about their views of writing in science during their school years the majority of student teachers said it was necessary to do it but that they were not interested and found it boring. The student teachers also described the way they approached writing in science when teaching: they used headings similar to those listed above; sometimes the actual headings were used. During the interviews students said they stuck to what they knew, especially in science, a subject they did not feel confident about. Even when students tried to introduce different means of recording and writing the class teacher sometimes insisted on 'proper scientific writing'.

Making writing in science more enjoyable and relevant for children is necessary if children are to be motivated and interested. A starting point is to ask why children write in science.

> Workbooks, folders or notebooks [are] for children to keep their own notes and make some record of the work. Some of it will be in the form of drawings and painting ... ways of ... avoiding the tedium of 'writing up' which spoils the excitement of science activities for so many children.
>
> (Harlen, 1988: 96)

To the suggestions above we could also add stories and poems and even embroidery, model-making and role-play. It was very encouraging that student teachers had given children so many opportunities to engage in the processes of scientific inquiry, to make predictions and to test them. Their pupils seemed to have had more experience than they usually did of practical work in science. This requires confidence to plan, organize and support effectively, a confidence the student teachers had successfully demonstrated. It was disappointing then that this confidence did not extend to planning innovative ways in which pupils could record and report their work in science, so that this essential dimension of a scientist's work appeared 'boring'.

Learning and teaching

One of the encouraging aspects of talking to the pupils about what they had learned was that they were enthusiastic and wanted to show off how much they knew. In fact, they wanted to find out more by asking extension questions about the work they had done. For example one of the groups at St Wilfrid's had been building circuits and finding out about conductors and insulators in the unit on electricity. While investigating which materials conducted electricity they had tried out virtually anything they could find in the room. They could explain the dangers of mains electricity as opposed to batteries and apply what they had learned to different situations.

At Hallam Road School with Miss Bailey, a Year 4 group studying separation techniques such as evaporation and filtration explained how they had used a sieve to separate sand and then filter paper to separate sand and water. This practical analogy enabled them to make the connection between the familiar sieve and the unfamiliar filter paper – that they were both used for the same purpose:

It works like a sieve. (Julie)
It has little holes and the water goes through but the sand doesn't. (Liz)

Further work on solutions produced methods for getting salt from seawater and separating salt and sand. The children were clearly able to apply their knowledge of filters to new situations.

Faced with imaginative investigations to pursue, the pupils had responded very well. At Eden School, in one of her lessons on separation techniques, Philippa Downes had asked her pupils to find out who wrote a forged cheque. The group discussed their assignment with animation. At the same school, another group who had been studying properties of matter described how,

We did a drama about solids, liquids and gases.

They had been asked to act as particles, demonstrating the various properties of matter. The lesson had gone very well and Philippa had received favourable feedback from her charges.

Any efforts that the students made to apply scientific concepts to real life and to use imaginative ideas such as drama in lessons were rewarded by an enthusiastic response from the pupils.

These pupils also commented appreciatively about how Philippa had regularly devised different worksheets for pupils of varying abilities. The pupils had really appreciated this and commented on it.

However, what pupils actually learn is not necessarily what their teachers think they have taught. Whilst a question may elicit the 'correct' answer, this may be because of the expectations of the teacher rather than due to pupils having explored the concept and developed their own understanding. One of the challenges that student teachers face is to use children's own experiences of everyday life as a resource and to start by finding out what their existing conceptual understanding is, then plan work based on these starting points. Our discussions with pupils provided little evidence that the predictions children were encouraged to make and the experiments and investigations they carried out originated from their own observations, questions and interests arising from their experience, or that students had tried to challenge/elicit pupils' existing understandings of the scientific concepts involved. There was little evidence that investigations carried out had not been pre-planned by the students, or that sometimes they did not work according to plan! This is understandable given the great emphasis placed on students' detailed planning, the subject knowledge, confidence and experience required to recognize teaching opportunities arising from within pupils' experiences and the need to know the pupils to do so. But scientific inquiries based on 'recipes' are only part-way along the route towards helping pupils to engage at their own levels in the genuine process of scientific inquiry.

Using computers

Computers can make it easier for children to record observations and create data bases which can be easily manipulated. Computers can be used for data logging, desktop publishing or internet use in science. All the pupils interviewed were asked whether they had used computers in science lessons with the student teachers. Children from only two classes said that they had, although others had used them in other subjects, especially in maths and English. One student had used interactive CD-ROMs which pupils thought had enhanced their learning and were very proud of their work, which was on display. The other student had used a simulation programme which the pupils had not liked as the graphics were poor.

So what does all this tell us?

Science for primary pupils is mainly concerned with the 'scientific process, with words such as "experimenting", "investigating" and "finding out"' (Johnston, 1996: 2). Doing science in primary school emphasizes process and the development of the skills of observing, classifying, identifying similarities and differences, planning, predicting and hypothesizing, measuring, communicating and recording. It is also about developing attitudes of curiosity, respect for evidence, respect and enjoyment of the living environment, and respect for each other. Practical work is a major way of developing these skills and attitudes, and, as we have seen, it can be motivating and enjoyable.

The student teachers apparently did more practical work with children than the class-teachers. This may be because teachers are under different pressures from students, their time for preparing practical sessions is limited, and they are not being assessed in the same ways as students. It may also be because another adult in the classroom allows teachers and students to work collaboratively in planning and supporting practical work in science.

Suggestions for:

Further reading

Feasey, R. and Goldsworthy, A. (1998) *Making Sense of Primary Science Investigations*, (second edn) Hatfield: Association for Science Education (ASE).

Hollins, M. and Whitby, V. (1998) *Progression in Primary Science*, London: David Fulton.

Newton, D. and Newton, L. (1998) *Co-ordinating Science Across the Primary School*, Lewes: Falmer Press.

Nuffield Primary Science S.P.A.C.E. (1997) *Understanding Science Ideas*, London: Collins Educational.

White, R. and Gunstone, R. (1992) *Probing Understanding*, Lewes: Falmer Press.

Further investigations

- Analyse your science lesson plans. Did you plan the activities to enable the development and assessment of particular skills?
- Review how you have asked pupils to record/write in science and consider different ways of doing this.
- Have you used ICT? What ICT resources are available in your school and how can you integrate their use into science classes?

Discussion with mentors in school

- How can you organize yourself and use the facilities in school to carry out as much practical work as possible?
- Many pupils are very confident about using PCs and the Net. How do teachers act as guides and how do they monitor their pupils while they are using the PCs to ensure effective learning?

Discussion on college-based courses

- How can you help children to understand what science is and how it differs from other subjects?
- How can teachers draw on and value children's and their own experiences in order to relate science to everyday life? How is drawing on this experience similar or different from using their beliefs and theories about science?

References

Association for Science Education (ASE) (1998) *Science 2000: Curriculum packs used in consultation*, Hatfield: ASE.

Association for Science Education (ASE) (1993) *The Place of Investigations in Science Education: Report from the Investigations in Science Task Group*, Hatfield: ASE.

DFE (1995) *Programmes of Study of the 1995 National Curriculum Science Order*, London: DFE.

Harlen, W. (ed.) (1988) *Primary Science: Taking the Plunge*, London: Heinemann.

Johnston, J. (1996) *Early Explorations in Science*, Buckingham: Open University Press.

Qualter, A. (1996) *Differentiated Primary Science*, Buckingham: Open University Press.

Riggs, A. and Hayhurst, A.M. (1995) 'Perceptions of science education: student teachers' reflections', paper presented at Science Education in Europe Inaugural Conference, Leeds University.

Web-sites

http://www.vtc.org.uk/
Information about all aspects of ICT and education plus software reviews.

http://vtc.ngfl.gov.uk/
Includes a meeting room to discuss issues of interest.

http://www.campus.bt.com/CampusWorld/pub/ext_tb.html
On-line discussion.

http://sol.ultralab.anglia.ac.uk/pages/schools_onLine/newsgroups/ – newsgroups
http://www.mailbase.ac.uk/lists/sci-ed-inet/
Discussion of the use of multimedia and especially the Internet for science education in the UK.

7 Technology

Wheels within wheels

Maureen Harrison

> To understand what a pupil understands will require a deep grasp of both the material to be taught and the processes of learning.
>
> (Shulman 1987: 19)

'Making things' is a substantial part of the design and technology curriculum. What do children think such projects are for? Why do student teachers design them? If there is a difference between children's and teachers' views, how might that difference be lessened?

Teachers need to be clear in their own minds about the purpose of a particular project. Events must be planned at the beginning of such projects: the teacher must explain the purpose, and then must make sure that each child has a clear understanding of the purpose. Inquiries carried out in the 1980s showed that there was often a disparity between the two (Bennett *et al.* 1984; Bennett and Kell 1989).

This is particularly pertinent to design and technology which involves the interaction between mind and hand. It was introduced as a new subject in the National Curriculum, and as Elizabeth Clayden and her colleagues (1994) suggest it is often difficult for teachers to plan work that is authentic to cultures which are unfamiliar to them.

Lee Shulman (1987) emphasizes that teachers need to design activities that encourage understanding. Shulman's model of teaching combines pedagogical reasoning and action and he proposes five distinct, though of course overlapping, events:

1 Preparation: becoming familiar with the available instructional materials;
2 Representation: designing ways to present the ideas, e.g. analogy, example, demonstration;
3 Instructional selections: choosing the teaching methods;
4 Adaptation (often called differentiation): adapting the presentation and teaching methods to individual children;
5 Evaluation and reflection: checking for understanding and misunderstanding during the lesson as well as formal assessments.

wheels, axles and body of the vehicle; selecting appropriate materials for the vehicle and reinforcing knowledge on how wheels and axles work.

- The initial presentation was well planned. It usually started with a discussion – an IDEA (investigative, disassembly and evaluative activity) such as examining a toy car to see how the wheels and axles had been attached and how they worked. This was followed by a focused practical task to give pupils, in the words of one student, 'ideas on how to use different materials'. In other words, modelling appropriate strategies.

- Tasks were suitably differentiated, formative assessments informed future planning and future intentions were more realistic.

What were the features of successful learning?

- Successful students' thorough planning and attention to resources resulted in many opportunities to learn.
- Lessons started with a brief recap of the previous session.
- The student teachers chose the 'subject' words to name and describe the equipment and materials carefully.
- Student-asked questions to assess progress about the concepts and skills taught, re-teaching if necessary before presenting new ideas and asking further questions to check for understanding. For example, when one student teacher discovered that some children were stuck, she brought the group together to *instruct* and re-teach in small steps. She provided contingent support for each pupil (Wood 1991). According to Tochon and Munby (1993: 374) 'novices rarely improvise but most experts do'.
- The process skills (exploring and investigating, organizing and planning, predicting and testing, evaluating, interpreting and communicating) were developed and exploited.
- The concept of wheels and axles was illustrated in many different contexts which provided opportunities for the pupils to engage with the subject discourse and observe how wheels are fixed and the axle moved freely in the axle holders.
- The presentations of the topic incorporated modelling ideas, asking questions that provided a structure for thinking and acting (cognitive structuring).
- Pupils were encouraged to clarify their ideas in conversation and so increase their understanding.
- Students talked to the children about their work and encouraged children to evaluate each other's work.

Some students recognized the importance of discussing and evaluating children's learning with them, both during and at the end of an activity.

One student teacher, Jane Lewis, remarked, 'I have a one-to-one conversation, but I always get the group together at the beginning and end of each session and tell them my overall feelings, whether I think they have worked really well or if there are little bits they could do better. We also share any work that I think one child has done particularly well. We will stop and have a look at that.' Another student, Carl Johnson, wrote 'I want the children to understand how and why vehicles move in relation to wheels and axles. They need to know that it isn't enough just to attach wheels to a model, either the wheels move freely or the wheels are fixed and the axle moves freely.'

Student teachers who were successful in scaffolding, engaged in the subject discourse which displayed knowledge of the key concepts and processes of design and technology. They transformed subject matter knowledge into appropriate activities. Tasks were structured and 'adapted' or 'differentiated' to meet the learning needs of the pupils and they identified and corrected any misconceptions by asking open-ended questions. For example, to clarify how an axle needs to move freely, one student teacher, Lesley Hall, asked, 'How have I stuck the wheel on the axle?' and John replied, 'You have made a hole'. Holding up a wooden axle, Lesley asked 'What would happen if I stuck this down?' Rizwana replied, 'It wouldn't move'. These tasks were clearly sequenced and built on the knowledge and skills previously learned.

Less successful lessons emphasized the smooth running of the activity to the neglect of pupil learning. Student teachers tended to concentrate on the finished outcome and the mechanical aspects of the activity, for example gluing and using sellotape, rather than the process and the pupils' learning. The children were often not clear about the purposes of the task: 'I'm making a car to take home'. Intentions were rather vague, the student teachers were unclear about the presentation of the task and the choice of materials was restricted. There was a profusion of lower-order questioning which neither assessed nor assisted. Although the use of praise fostered a positive atmosphere questions neither helped children to see the purpose of an activity nor assessed what they had learned from it. James said 'I found a box and the sticks, I cutted the stick and glued it down'; he was happily unaware of his failure to make it move!

In the less successful lessons, student teachers tended to focus on what the children would do, not what they wanted them to learn. They provided so much support for the activity itself that the pupils did little more than follow instructions. Asif said 'Can I have four Smartie tubes?'. The student teacher replied, 'You don't need four, you need two Smartie tubes and two big tubes' although the student teacher had not demonstrated how the two small Smartie tubes would fit inside the two large cylinders to create movement. The task became a routine activity that was easily achievable, whereas actual problem-solving tasks are high on risk and ambiguity.

Omitting challenging tasks means limiting pupils' actual learning. Lessons ended abruptly – there was no time for evaluation or feedback. As long as pupils enjoyed the work and remained interested, student teachers felt the sessions had been successful. Pupils may have been learning but the question still remains, was this what the student teacher had actually intended them to learn?

Knowing when to intervene, when to 'help' and how is gained by experience with children and also the opportunity for student teachers to reflect on the occasions when such interventions were helpful to them or would have been helpful. Bliss (1996) reports that teachers appear to think explaining the whole task would give the game away. Constable (1995) found many teachers believed designing and making is about discovery, and showing pupils how to do it should not interrupt the creative process. She argues the skills are the 'foundation' of design and technological capability and the skills of cutting, shaping and joining should be taught didactically if necessary. Moreover, the processes such as predicting, modifying or evaluating should be demonstrated. Evaluating is at the heart of designing and making but quite often pupils' evaluations go unnoticed. Testing enables pupils to find out if they have solved the problem to their satisfaction, in this case how well their vehicle moves. As Rizwana (Year 2) explained, 'I need to check it running down the ramp'. Encouraging pupils to talk about their work helps them to identify problems and how they might be overcome and at the same time helps the teachers to assess pupil progress. Emma said, 'I'm thinking how to make it move better'. In design and technology, pupils need to develop the meta-cognitive skills of reflecting on a task that can be done through the evaluation process.

In design and technology, pupils are expected to assume an active role in their learning. Intervention strategies by the teacher either to teach new skills, or extend the pupils' thinking can enhance pupils' competencies in active learning and in being aware of their own learning.

Suggestions for:

Further reading

Whilst the following books do not refer specially to design and technology, they provide useful information to student teachers on how children's learning may be supported.

Bennett, B. and Carré, C. (1993) *Learning to Teach*, London: Routledge.
This specifically looks at student teachers on a postgraduate course as they learn about the craft of teaching. It analyses students' work using Shulman's model of pedagogical reasoning.

Edwards, A. and Collison, J. (1996) *Mentoring and Developing Practice in Primary Schools*, Milton Keynes: Open University Press.

Provides a wealth of information to support both students and mentors in schools and cites five aspects of teacher knowledge.

Muschamp, Y. (1996) 'Pupil self-assessment', in A. Pollard (ed.) *Readings for Reflective Teaching in the Primary School*, London: Cassell.

Considers involving children in their own assessment, which is important in the evaluation process in design and technology.

Pollard, A. (1997) *Reflective Teaching in the Primary School*, London: Cassell, pp. 249–267 addresses the various forms of classroom communication and the issues involved.

Tharp, R. and Gallimore, R. (1988) *Rousing Minds to Life*, Cambridge: Cambridge University Press.

Provides details of the four stages of assisted performance and the means of assisting performance.

Further investigation

- Consider how you create a balance between the processes of action and reflection. List ways in which you can ascertain what the children are thinking and planning (for example drawing, talking, painting, modelling, writing). Revise your planning if necessary.
- Ask a colleague to observe you during a lesson and to note instances when you intervene to promote children's learning using the following categories: explanation, demonstration, questioning, teaching new skills. Discuss these notes after the lesson and consider other possible opportunities.

Discussion on college-based courses

- Discuss with others and list problems which you anticipate children may have in relation to a particular lesson plan for technology; make a parallel list of possible scaffolding strategies.
- Share and evaluate examples of ways in which you have assessed and recorded children's learning in technology. Have you assessed conceptual understanding and skills?

Discussion with mentors in school

- Was the task appropriate to your stated intentions?
- Was your presentation (explanation, demonstration or instruction) accurate and suitable?
- Were your tasks suitable for pupils' differing capabilities?

References

Bennett, N. and Kell, J. (1989) *A Good Start? Four-Year-Olds in Infant Schools*, Oxford: Basil Blackwell.

Bennett, N., Desforges, C., Cockburn, A. and Wilkinson, B. (1984) *The Quality of Pupil Learning Experiences*, London: Lawrence Erlbaum Associates.

Bliss, J., Askew, M. and Macrae, S. (1996) 'Effective teaching and learning: scaffolding revisited', *Oxford Review of Education* 22(1): 37–61.

Bruner, J. S. (1996) *Towards a Theory of Instruction*, Cambridge MA: Harvard University Press.

Clayden, E., Desforges, C., Mills, C. and Rawson, W. (1994) 'Authentic activity and learning', *British Journal of Educational Studies* 42 (2): 163–173.

Constable, H. J. (1995) 'Design and technology and information technology' in A. Anning (ed.) *A National Curriculum for the Early Years*, Buckingham: Open University Press.

Edwards, A. and Collison, J. (1996) *Mentoring and Developing Practice in Primary Schools*, Buckingham: Open University Press.

Pollard, A., Broadfoot, P., Croll, P. and Abbot, D. (1994) *Changing English Primary Schools? The Impact of the Education Reform Act at Key Stage 1*, London: Cassell.

Shulman, L.S. (1987) 'Knowledge and teaching: Foundations of the New Reform', *Harvard Educational Review* 57(1): 1–22.

Tharp, R. and Gallimore, R. (1988) *Rousing Minds to Life*, Cambridge: Cambridge University Press.

Tochon, F. and Munby, H. (1993) 'Novice and expert teachers' time epistemology: a wave function from didactics to pedagogy', *Teacher and Teacher Education* 9(2): 205–218.

Vygotsky, L. (1978) *Mind in Society*, Cambridge MA: Harvard University Press.

Wood, D. (1991) 'Aspects of teaching and learning', in P. Light, S. Sheldon and M. Woodhead (eds) *Learning to Think*, London: Routledge/Open University.

8 1066 and all that!

Pupil misconceptions in history

Mike Huggins

Children's talk and writing often reveals discrepancies between teachers' learning objectives set out in lesson plans and what children have actually learned. This is particularly true of history. For example, let us begin by considering four instances of pupils' misconceptions and misunderstandings recorded by Helena Trotter. The topic was the Victorians, taught to a Year 5 class.

The first was not an important mistake, but one needing to be corrected: Gary wrote carefully about 'The Great Expedition' of 1851 instead of the Great Exhibition. The reason for misspelling was unclear, but Gary's work was about the Great Exhibition.

History teaching often relies partly on textbooks. But even more able pupils can be misled by print as well as informed by it, especially when working independently. Sarah had read about Victorian board schools but her textbook did not explain the term. She concluded that they were called board schools 'because the teachers all used blackboards'. Helena Trotter provided another textbook which had more extensive information. Ralph had read in his textbook that from the 1880s the development of the camera meant that many photographs survived, and so he was sure that 'there weren't any photographs until 1880. They just drew pictures'. Even when he was shown photographs (in the same textbook) clearly dated in the 1860s and 1870s, it took some time to convince him. The same class had been examining a range of Victorian artefacts. One group discussed the 'dolly', used for agitating washing.

TEACHER: What do you think this is?
JANE: [reading a small sticker on the object] It's a dolly.
TEACHER: Can you describe it to me?
[Stephanie describes it.]
TEACHER: So what do you think it was used for?
JANE: I think it might have been to put clothes on and dress it up.
STEPHANIE: But the rest of the things are for washing. I think people used it
    to hang their clothes on when they were drying. You would hang them
    on these bits here and you would twizzle it round to dry the clothes.

At this point Helena Trotter showed the children photographs, some of which provided a context for the 'dolly'. After a discussion the children were able to explain how a dolly was used for agitating dirty laundry.

Another kind of misunderstanding occurred when Helena attempted to use a novel to personalize the past. After careful thought she chose Teresa Thomlinson's *The Flither Pickers* (1987), a moving story about women's lives in the fishing industry of the north-east. There were Victorian photographs of the fishing quays at Whitby, taken by the contemporary photographer Frank Meadow Sutcliffe. Some of the less-able pupils believed that Liz Weford and other characters in the story were real people, even though they understood the general difference between fictional characters and real people. Their confusion came about partly because of the photographs of real people and partly because Sutcliffe was one of the characters in the story. Helena recognized the children's confusion and developed work during the Literacy Hour to discuss real and fictional characters in 'stories'. These misunderstandings were all remedied without a major rethink of lesson plans. But some pupil errors and misconceptions are more serious and in recognizing and identifying them some key questions are useful. How well do primary-school children of different ages understand the specialized concepts which we use in teaching history? What sorts of misconceptions are common? Why do these misconceptions occur? How can they be corrected?

These are important questions because finding out about the past involves understanding and using specialized vocabulary. This may be special names historians use to describe historical periods (the Victorians), particular events (the Great Exhibition), past institutions (board schools), or artefacts no longer used (dolly). Finding out about the past also involves particular kinds of inquiry. How were things in the past similar to and different from today? How have they changed and why? These depend on understanding language used to describe and measure the passing of time (earlier, later, decade, century). Because so much about the past cannot be known we must use language of hypothesis, and probability; ('I think it might have been to put the clothes on'), to explain our reasons (because . . .) and to find further evidence which contradicts or supports our explanations. Sarah found more books about board schools which contested her assumption; Ralph needed to check the photograph dates; Jane's and Stephanie's inferences about the dolly were corroborated by the photographs and discussion with the student gave them the vocabulary to explain this. I wonder whether Helena Trotter herself knew that Frank Meadow Sutcliffe's photographs were in fact artificially posed and did not reflect the reality of life in Whitby at the time. Interpretations of the past, distinctions between fact and fiction are rarely simple. On the whole though Helena recognized and responded effectively to her pupils' misunderstandings and so was able to use them in planning their future learning. Whilst looking at what pupils have achieved comes first, a focus on errors in pupils' history work helps you establish progress made and decide where to go next (Hughes 1998).

What sorts of misconceptions do children have and where do they get them from?

Circular 4/98 (DfEE 1998) identifies common errors in both English and mathematics. We know much less about common errors and misconceptions in the foundation subjects. Research on history misconceptions is still limited. We are still exploring what pupils actually can or cannot do in history at different stages. Even those who have made the teaching of history their lifetime study cannot confidently detail the steps which children make as they learn, and even less the mistakes they make. As history education researchers admit, research has been piecemeal and insufficient (Cooper 1995; Knight 1996) compared to the work on the core subjects, although there has been some limited exploration (e.g. Lee *et al.* 1996; Levstik and Barton 1996; Pendry *et al.* 1997).

Nevertheless a great deal of information can be obtained from the actual observation of history lessons and the scrutiny of pupils' work. As we shall see later, many of the structured tasks which we already carry out with small groups of pupils can help us to explore pupil misconceptions and respond effectively.

Limited knowledge

Primary-school pupils are immature and inevitably have a limited knowledge base. Many pupil misconceptions are simply due to a lack of knowledge. Florence Jacobson in introducing her Non-European Study Unit on Benin, used concept mapping to find out what children knew about West Africa. This revealed a paucity of knowledge, as well as some prejudices. One child wrote 'not a lot of nice people', 'monkeys', 'people who do bad things'; another 'a poor hot country'; and a third 'hot, trees with fruits on, black people, houses made out of trees, camels'. Florence modified her lesson plan in order to address these misunderstandings and prejudices. She deliberately first used modern material on West Africa (drawn from a children's education TV series) to show the 'modernity' of life there, and in looking at Benin, she took a very positive multicultural approach to demonstrate that Benin and the Portuguese civilizations were of similar power and status at the time. She made comparisons with Tudor Britain, which the pupils had earlier studied.

Out-of-school influences

Pupils do not get all their historical ideas from the schools. Biased, incomplete or inaccurate views of the past which they encounter in family conversations, or through entertainment, sources, cartoons, films, drama, can lead to prejudices if not discussed and contested. As I talked to groups of five or six children and asked them what history is, what they know about the past, and how they knew about it, this soon became clear. Jason (Year 3) was sure that the Germans and Japanese were 'the enemy' and that Britain was still at war with Germany. The Germans 'dropped bombs on people' and the Japanese 'tortured you'. Jason had not studied 'Britain Since 1930', but he did have a great-granddad! All pupils attempt to understand the world about them, and develop their language and concepts about history, from a range of sources. Their ideas will often differ from accepted history, although by the age of six or seven some pupils already have a good idea of the past. But even at the end of Key Stage 1 these children will have gained much of their historical knowledge and have developed their conceptual framework of history from a range of sources outside school. Some will have visited museums, others will have gained most of their understanding from their families, from television and from films. Grandparents are often quoted. School work, fictional and non-fictional books about history, may play a much more secondary role. Teachers are aware of this. As one remarked, 'the community around children is an intrinsic part of their lives. It is something to use and build upon, not something to ignore'.

Changing attitudes and values

People in the past often had attitudes and values different from our own, for many reasons. We can never know how they thought or felt. It is only possible to conjecture how they might have felt from what we know of the times in which they lived, the traces of those times which remain, pictures, artefacts, writing, and because we all share some common human attitudes. It is very difficult for young children, with limited knowledge, for whom understanding the viewpoints of others is a developing skill, to understand attitudes other than their own. Changing attitudes to fashion illustrate this in a simple way. We all understand the idea of fashion, but fashions change.

Tammy Wilson was discussing a pair of 1970s flares. She asked her pupils what they thought of them. One pupil said 'old-fashioned'. 'Do you think the person who wore them in 1972 thought they were old fashioned?', Tammy asked. The class agreed that they would have done. This made Tammy realize that the question was more complex than she thought. She went on to discuss fashion in 1972, why floral shirts for men, velvet flares, platform shoes and long hair were fashionable; to compare these clothes with fashions today, how they are similar and different and why fashions change.

Anachronisms

By far the largest category of misconception is the anachronism. Using aircraft to defeat the Spanish Armada, injections to combat the spread of the Black Plague, or believing that Tudor houses had gas-fired central heating are examples of the sorts of responses which teachers have experienced and which more insightful teaching can eliminate. Television sets and electric lights are a feature of many pictures of past times drawn by Key Stage 1 pupils, and show how difficult it is for young children to imagine an age without the household technologies that have always been part of their own lives.

Sensitive teaching can however address such issues over time. Rob, a Year 1 child in a group discussing a portrait of Henry VIII, made sensible suggestions about why it might have been painted and why the king was portrayed as he was, but he also thought that after it had been painted Henry might have watched television. Hazel Mangolies, the trainee student, praised Rob for his good ideas, but then went on to use further questioning and introduce further Tudor pictures to enable the pupils to begin to conclude that television and indeed electricity were yet to be invented.

Many of the errors that trainee teachers spot fairly easily are associated with chronology in some way, most especially in pupils' use of chronological language. This is often an indicator of conceptual confusion. Many younger pupils do not understand words and phrases associated with time. Other pupils misuse terms such as 'yesterday', 'last year', 'century', 'ancient' or 'decade' well into Key Stage 2. Scott, a Year 3 pupil, for example, was discussing a Victorian hot-water bottle.

TRAINEE: What do you think it is?
SCOTT: It's for holding water. There's the hole for putting water in.
TRAINEE: Is it old or new?
SCOTT: It looks old.
TRAINEE: This is an old hot-water bottle, for keeping you warm at night. Would you have liked to use one of these?
SCOTT: No, it looks too hard and I don't think it would get very warm. It was probably used in caves when people had no beds to sleep in. A thousand years ago, or a million years ago.

Scott is beginning to use appropriate terminology and shows some evidence of reasoning, but although he uses words like hundred and million he does not understand what the words represent.

The language of the calendar system needs to be taught. A common problem for pupils is the misassociation of year dates (1066; 1939) with century dates (eleventh century, twentieth century). BC and AD dates can cause further confusion. The meaning of abbreviations such as BC, BCE and AD must be carefully taught. One child believed that AD stood for 'after death' – so Jesus lived for a very short time!

Dealing with history misconceptions

Misconceptions and or misunderstandings can be identified in scrutiny of pupils' written work, and in other ways in which they represent the past (model-making, drawings, role-play) and through questioning and discussion.

First, misconceptions must be recognized. If the teacher's knowledge and understanding is weak pupil errors will be overlooked, and may even be perpetuated.

Second, we need to know how pupil errors have come about. If some of our teaching has contributed to or exacerbated pupil errors we need to be able to recognize that in our evaluations of lessons, and alter our teaching style appropriately.

Third, we need to provide the history scaffolding to remedy them (Cooper 1993; Huggins 1997). A useful approach which gives better focus to future medium-term planning at the start of a Study Unit is to use concept mapping. The maps provide evidence of initial misconceptions. Knowledge of these can then be built into the planning process and used later, once the Unit is well underway, to help pupils play an active role in correcting them.

A combination of open and closed questions, sometimes done orally and sometimes written down, helps to draw out pupils' existing knowledge and ideas. One trainee teacher, Brian Foster, had introduced his Key Stage 2 pupils to Tudor portraits, but the groups just studied one portrait. Although the plenary session at the end of the session was supposed to allow comparisons, this was not particularly effective. His questioning revealed that some pupils thought that these individual portraits were the only record of these people, whilst others thought that the pictures were accurate representations of the people concerned. This meant that he had to modify his planning and introduce two activities. First, he obtained a range of pictures of Henry VIII so that pupils could compare and contrast and begin to get a sense of the ageing process and change over time in costume and portraiture presentation of the king. Second, he used written sources to reveal, for instance, that Henry had smallpox scars but that these were not shown. This helped Brian's pupils to understand that portraits are intended to convey particular messages, and that these messages may sometimes be contradictory.

Where misconceptions do not emerge until the end of a lesson, in a plenary session or in written work, then good follow-up planning is necessary. A common misconception for pupils learning the skills of historical inquiry was to believe that historical statements in a book or made by the teacher are necessarily true, and they often failed to recognize that views needed to be justified by evidence. Jacquelyn Field set up collaborative work in groups to help children to learn the kind of questions to ask about the artefacts she had brought into school and the ways they might be answered. She wanted to encourage the pupils to make inferences: what were they, how were they made and used, by whom, and why? By careful questioning she was able to encourage pupils to do this, to justify their arguments and compare them to the views of others. In her planning she tried to think through what children might know, what they might be able to guess and made lists of questions to ask and the vocabulary she wanted to get the children to employ. Following this use of appropriate scaffolding she reported that:

> The children were really inquisitive about the artefacts and discussed them ever so well and asked relevant questions that we could explore further to find out more. I was particularly pleased that the children used 'because' much more than they had. I had wanted them to use 'therefore' as well but that was not so successful so I need to come back to that.

Where discussion required pupils to articulate their ideas by explaining, predicting and using historical evidence to justify their statements there was far less chance of misconceptions developing. For history is not a body of factual knowledge which can be learned. Finding out about the past involves asking particular kinds of questions, and particular methods of answering them, using specialized language. In doing so pupils' misconceptions are revealed and can be addressed.

Suggestions for:

Further reading

Some of the most interesting work on pupils' developing concepts of evidence, accounts, cause and rational understanding has been carried out by Project CHATA (Concepts of History and Teaching Approaches). Details can be found in Lee *et al.* (1996).

A good account of American pupils' chronological thinking can be found in Levstik and Barton (1996). Pendry *et al.* (1997) describe a range of investigations into secondary pupils' misconceptions.

Further investigations

Structured approaches which examine the preconceptions which pupils may have include:

- brainstorming by pupils – individual spider diagrams or concept maps *or* free writing of words associated with a topic

One trainee teacher, in collecting pupils' impressions of the Vikings during her preparatory visit to the school in order to plan a Study Unit on the

Romans, Anglo-Saxons and Vikings, obtained a predominantly warlike picture of them, which emphasized their raids, with no real reference to settlement or to their everyday life. Her pupils listed 'they liked fighting', 'attacking and killing people', 'they didn't care who they killed', 'they murdered everyone', 'wooden boats', 'helmets with horns on', 'invaders', 'they came over the sea'. In her subsequent teaching, she was careful to spend time on Viking settlement and its legacy and on everyday life, and to stress that settlement did not necessarily depend on conflict, but could also be peaceable.

- giving pupils mixed vocabulary both relevant and irrelevant to a topic to circle and discuss

In one class a group of Year 5 pupils had been asked to build up a glossary of concept words on the computer, in alphabetical order, associated with their topic on Ancient Greece, with explanations of each of the words chosen. When the trainee took the class again the following year she gave them a range of specialized concepts they had learnt as part of their work on Ancient Greece to see how many her pupils could sort and recognize.

You could also try pupil activities such as:

- underlining true/false sentences about a topic;
- having three stereotyped pictures about a topic to rank in order of accuracy and to discuss.

Discussion with mentors in school

- Ask your mentor for examples of how s/he has had to interpret pupils' responses and recognize pupils' historical understandings and misunderstandings. How did this inform later instructional decisions?
- Find examples of misconceptions in pupils' work and discuss with your mentor possible ways forward.

Discussion on college-based courses

- Make a list of the first four key elements of historical inquiry identified in the National Curriculum for History. In small groups discuss from your own experience examples of pupil misconceptions related to each one.
- Choose one and set it in its teaching context then try to work out how you would address this in a subsequent lesson.

References

Cooper, H. (1993) 'Removing the scaffolding: a case study investigating how whole class teaching can lead to effective peer group discussion', *Curriculum Journal* 4(3): 385–401.

Cooper, H. (1995) *The Teaching of History in Primary Schools*, London: David Fulton (3rd edn 2000).

DfEE (1998) Circular 4/98, *Teaching: High Status, High Standards*, London: Teacher Training Agency.

Huggins, M. (1997) 'Helping primary pupils access archive material in the context of Tudor local history', *Teaching History* 87: 31–36.

Hughes, M. (1998) 'Research on teaching and learning and its implications for teacher education', in R. Guyver and R. Phillips (eds), *Preparation for Teaching History; Research and Practice*, London: University College of St Martin.

Knight, P. (1996) 'Research and the improvement of school history', *Advances in Research in Teaching* 6: 19–50.

Lee, P.J., Dickinson, A.K., and Ashby, R. (1996) 'Children making sense of history', *Education 3–13* 24(1): 13–19.

Levstik, L.S. and Barton, K. (1996) 'They still use some of their past; historical salience in elementary children's chronological thinking', *Journal of Curriculum Studies* 28(3): 531–576.

Pendry, A. E., Atha, J., Carden, S., Courtney, L., Keogh, C. and Ruston, K. (1997) 'Pupil misconceptions in history', *Teaching History* 86: 18–20.

Thomlinson, T. (1987) *The Flither Pickers*, London: Julia MacRae Books.

Vygotsky, L.S. (1962) *Thought and Language*, trans. E. Hanfmann and G. Vakar, Cambridge MA: MIT Press.

9 Literacy activities
Purposeful tasks or ways of keeping busy?

Sam Twiselton

How do student teachers help children to become effective readers and writers?

Why is this an important question?

> Really I was just concentrating on getting it done.
>> Anna Goldman, First Block Placement

> That was to help them with verbs because that was next.
>> Andrew Burns, Final Block Placement

> I wanted them to think about story structures – that would help them with their prediction.
>> Martha O'Brien, Final Block Placement

Anna, Andrew and Martha made these comments as I talked to them after each had just finished teaching an English lesson. Our conversations supported the not unexpected consensus of researchers, tutors and student teachers themselves that student teachers' perceptions of what is involved in effective English teaching changes. In the beginning (as exemplified by Anna) student teachers concentrate on the activity. As they move towards the end of their training student teachers have learned that good English teaching is about much more than completing a specific task. While learning activities remain important for experienced teachers, it is because they are just that – vehicles for learning. The learning is important, not the activity alone. This chapter examines the consequences of the differing ways these three student teachers viewed their English lessons in the light of what the children understood as a result of the lessons.

Anna Goldman

I observed Anna's class when she was half way through her First Block Placement (towards the end of her first year of training). St James' school is large and urban with a varied catchment. She was teaching a small group of Year 1 children how to play a game: pictures of food had to be matched to written labels. At the end of the lesson Anna and I talked about the lesson – her main focus, her role and what she thought was involved in effective English teaching.

The most striking thing about Anna's comments was that her main focus was to get through the lesson and complete the game. She described the lesson in terms of the activity but did not refer to what the children were learning.

> They had to take it in turns to turn over a card from a pile of single pictures and labels and see if they could match it with their board. That was it really.

Her role was to oversee the activity and ensure that it went smoothly:

> My role was organization – make sure they went in turns. I went clockwise. Give encouragement. I kept the group small so they wouldn't have to wait long for their turn. It was very important to keep them motivated. Especially that, because it was a competition. They thought it was a race and I kept trying to reassure them that it wasn't, that the next person was also going to finish.

Anna judged the lesson a success because children were on task, there was a concrete product at the end. When I asked her what areas she needed to improve on in her English teaching, Anna commented:

> Just ideas really, I'm always looking for good ideas.

This view was totally understandable at this point in her training. Student teachers are expected to 'perform' at the same time as they learn. Performing in front of a class full of children (with mentor and tutor in evidence as well) can seem not so different from standing on a stage pulling rabbits out of a hat. Early on, having enough 'tricks' is what makes you feel you're getting it right. It is natural, at any stage, to be desperate for quick ideas for practical activities that will give you confidence and purpose.

Unfortunately (as most student teachers learn over the course of their training), 'tricks' are not enough to guarantee effective literacy learning. Andrew (after almost four years of training) understood this.

Andrew Burns

I observed Andrew teaching Year 4 children during a Literacy Hour on his Final Block Placement in Petersgate, a medium-sized school in a largely middle-class area. His aim was to have the children identify verbs. He used a poem with the whole class and then moved on to group work; each group had a different poem. Andrew's main concern was to cover the objectives that the class teacher had suggested.

> I had to do the reading so they could go on to look at the verbs, that was what Mrs Simpson wanted.

He was concerned (like Anna) with motivation:

> I wanted to keep them going – not to lose them.

and with control:

> If you lose their attention, that's when they start to play you up – I've lost them before and it's a nightmare.

Unlike Anna, one of Andrew's main concerns was to follow the plan and cover the objectives.

> I had all these things to cover and I had to keep it going.

Like Anna, Andrew felt he needed lesson ideas, but he related them to learning objectives:

> There's so much to cover. We just need lots of ideas of how to do it all.

The big difference between Andrew and Anna is that he showed that he saw a purpose to the task beyond simply wanting to get it done. His comments were generally focused on learning outcomes. However, he had little confidence in why they were important. The learning objectives were provided by the class teacher and the National Literacy Strategy. Andrew appeared to have a limited understanding of how they would help children's literacy in broader terms. Although clear about the purpose of the lesson – knowing about verbs – why children needed to know about verbs, and how they could usefully apply that knowledge were not part of Andrew's understanding.

> I needed to get some 'word level' in because we hadn't done any yet. That was to help them with verbs because that was next.

Although near the end of his training Andrew had learned to focus much more on learning objectives, it was worrying that he seemed so unconfident about the purpose of those objectives. Learning objectives taken from a given curriculum without being fully understood are not enough.

Objectives are not separate entities – 'chunks' of information that get piled on top of each other. Jerome Bruner (1966) uses the phrase, 'the structures of subjects' to describe the underlying principles that relate all the component concepts. English lessons over the primary school years should be an on-going process.

For example, story and poetry writing will begin in Reception and still be taking place in Year 6. Children will be expected to achieve a cumulative awareness of the structures, devices and vocabulary which make their writing more effective. They will also be developing an increasing awareness of what constitutes effective writing in other contexts. Teachers need to be able to help pupils to view reading and writing in specific, focused ways in order to develop skills and concepts that will be transferred on to other occasions.

Martha O'Brien was much closer to understanding her teaching in this way.

Martha O'Brien

Martha was a fourth-year student teacher when I observed her, halfway through her Final Block Placement. She was teaching a Literacy Hour to Year 2 children in Victoria Park, a large urban, multicultural school. She helped the children to plan the setting, characters and basic plot for a class story, using a Big Book story, *Elmer*, by David McKee (1989), as a starting point. The children then began to plan their own group stories using planning worksheets.

Martha's comments after the lesson are strikingly different from the others. She was more focused on the concepts and skills the children needed to learn. The tasks she assigned were designed to promote these skills and concepts. Typically, they linked one concept to another one taught previously. Examples include:

> I wanted them to think about story structures – that would help them with their prediction.

> Helping them think about the main characters was really important. That's the key. If you know the characters it helps you write a good story and it helps you when you are reading too.

This clarity of purpose also came through strongly when Martha was teaching. Because she had a firm understanding of why the learning outcomes were important, she was able to follow this through by helping children in specific, focused ways:

> Why should he behave like that?
> If you put that there it makes more sense.

Martha also acknowledged that she still had a lot to learn.

> I get frustrated that I can sometimes see where they are going wrong
> but I'm not sure of the best way to help them.

Anna, Andrew and Martha looked at their teaching from different perspectives. What might be the possible consequences for the children's learning?

The children

I interviewed a small number of children shortly after each lesson. My aim was to highlight possible patterns in the way the children viewed the tasks each of the student teachers had prepared. I reminded the children of key things that had happened or that the student teacher had said, using a range of 'prompts' including quotes from the student teacher, resources that had been used and pieces of children's work. Typical questions were: 'Tell me about this.' 'What was happening here?'

As one would expect, the children made a number of often conflicting comments. However, there were distinct trends to these comments and these are now examined in detail.

Anna's Year 1 children

Two clear trends emerged from this interview. The first can best be described as: 'We were doing it because it's fun'. However, few of Anna's children added any other ideas. Typical examples include:

> It's just what we like doing.
> She makes it fun for us.

The second trend was a pattern of perceiving the tasks in terms of 'because the teacher wanted us to'. While many of the children expressed a desire to follow instructions, a noticeable number of statements did not include any other reasons, even though they were prompted to do so. Their relationship with Anna was clearly important:

> Miss Goldman likes it if we do that.
> It's just because that's what she said.

Andrew's Year 4 children

Andrew's children (although older) actually replicated the trends found in Anna's Year 2 children. Many said they did the tasks because they were told.

One more strong pattern emerged. This could be described as 'because it's what we do at school'. They saw the lesson and its component parts as just 'something that you do', but with no apparent purpose beyond 'this is what school is all about'. Typical examples include:

If we do it then we can choose.
That's life – it's what we were told.

Martha's Year 2 children

Some comments fitted with the trends apparent in Anna's and Andrew's children, but there were two further patterns that are highly significant: it will help us do other things in school and it will help us do other things in general.

We were doing it because it will help us to do other things in school

Comments revealed some understanding that the tasks were helping them to develop knowledge and skills that would be useful on other classroom occasions:

It will help us next time we do something like this.
It helps us understand other stories.

It will help us to do other things in general

These comments made links with something beyond purely classroom-based activities. The children had some understanding that knowledge and skills being developed were of general use. Sometimes this was specifically related to the future, at other times to the present:

Doing that sort of thing helps you write better.
It might help you read when you are a mummy.
It helps you think about what makes the writing good.
It makes me think about my reading, like when I'm reading my other books too.

Comparing the comments from children taught by the three student teachers, the clearest difference is between Martha and the other two. In both Anna's and Andrew's lessons there seems to be a relationship between their focus on 'getting it done' and the children's failure to see an autonomous purpose to the task.

This relates closely to an article by Clayden *et al.* (1994) where the nature of classroom experience in a number of studies is explored. While classrooms are frequently very busy places, with both pupils and teachers working extremely hard, the activities simply help children with the 'working practices of the classroom. .... How to do work, how to be neat, how to finish on time (or sometimes how to spin the work out) and how to tidy away'. In other words, the children learn how to manage classroom work but do not develop concepts and skills that go beyond it. The pattern of comments from the children taught by Anna and Andrew clearly corresponds to this type of potentially superficial activity.

Schooling is based on the idea that children learn things there they will need to know and do elsewhere; they need to be able to transfer what they learn from one situation to another. Student teachers, in order to become effective literacy teachers, need to develop English teaching strategies that help children with concepts and skills which can be transferred beyond the immediate task. They need to view the task in broader terms, to understand the concepts and skills that underpin it and to relate this to other tasks and areas of understanding. For example, *Rosie's Walk* by Pat Hutchins (1973) is structured around a series of near misses, where the fox nearly gets Rosie. If children can be helped to link this pattern to similar patterns in other stories they have developed an understanding of cause and effect, motives and rules in stories with consistent dependable characters, which move steadily towards a predictable outcome; stories such as *Goldilocks*, *The Billy Goats Gruff* and *Peter Rabbit*, in which rigid rules apply, but those in peril ultimately emerge safely. Another example is identifying the initial sounds in words. If children who have played a game involving the letter 's' are helped to use their newly developed recognition of its sound and appearance to identify words beginning with 's' in the context of a text, once again the knowledge reaches well beyond the initial experience.

Pupils need to see the purpose and meaning of a task beyond simply getting it done, or because they've been told to do it. These inexperienced student teachers had not yet developed their own understanding of the concepts children need to develop their English proficiency and so could not teach in ways that helped the children move beyond the immediate task. This is to be expected in the early stages of teacher training when class management is the priority. What matters is that this is only a transient stage.

Martha had helped the Year 2 children to understand that what they were learning had application elsewhere. How did she manage to convey this understanding? On paper her lesson plan looked quite similar to Andrew's. Both had appropriate, focused learning objectives and had thought through the detail of how they would be covered. The difference was not in their planning, but in their teaching.

Andrew demonstrated that even near the end of training it is possible to be proficient on paper without being as effective in implementation. Although his teaching was clearly focused, and the skills and concepts he meant to cover appropriate, Andrew did not have the confidence (and perhaps the subject knowledge) to explain the underlying framework of the tasks he assigned.

It's in the Literacy Strategy, that's why I did it – I probably wouldn't have otherwise.

This was reflected in his teaching strategies: he did little to help the children in specific ways and was more likely to give general encouragement than to explain specific concepts or skills.

In her teaching Martha moved beyond the 'script' to a point where she understood what she was doing so well that she could scaffold the children's learning on a moment-by-moment basis. Her teaching strategies demonstrated the same sense of purpose and focus as her discussion. This was particularly clear in the specific and targeted help given to individuals.

Think about the story – what has just happened?
Where else have you seen that word?

The children referred to specific things Martha had done or said which were helpful:

She showed me how to cover up bits of the word.
She helped us to use the bits of the story we liked to help us make our own story.

David Wood (1988) produced some useful insights into what makes teaching effective. He looked particularly at pre-school children and how they learned from their mothers. He asked the mothers to teach their children simple tasks like building constructions. He noticed that the mothers who transferred their knowledge most effectively were those who responded to the actions of the children on a 'moment-by-moment' basis. Similarly, an activity works well when the teacher responsively scaffolds the learner through it, by making what David Wood describes as contingent interventions. This means identifying what a child does not yet understand then working out how to help the youngster move on.

This study supports the findings of a more extensive inquiry carried out by François Tochon and Hugh Munby (1993) – a comparative study of novice and expert teachers. The expert teachers adapted continuously to the children's performance as it unfolded while the novices stuck to the lesson plan through thick and thin. The task itself takes over and the learning it is supposed to promote is neglected.

How the teacher views the task will determine how effectively s/he helps the children learn from it. How the children view the task will help to determine how well they succeed in transferring the learning from that occasion to other occasions so they read, write and talk with increasing insight and skill.

Clearly 'novice' and 'expert' are not either/or categories – they exist on a continuum. What is important is that student teachers, with the help of mentors, tutors and children, can make *visible* progress along this continuum.

Suggestions for:

Further reading

Wray, D. and Medwell, J. (1998) *Teaching English in Primary Schools*, London: Letts Educational.

Lloyd, P., Mitchell, H. and Monk, J. (1999) *The Literacy Hour and Language Knowledge*, London: David Fulton.

Bunting, R. (1997) *Teaching about Language in the Primary Years*, London: David Fulton.

Further investigations

List the key concepts and skills identified in the learning outcomes you plan for when you teach English. For each one, think about *specific* ways it should help children in other areas (within and outside English and within and outside the classroom).

Example

1   Understanding of the sequence in the story
    This will help them to predict story lines and words that fit with them. Also it will help them plan their own stories.
2   Understanding of the main character
    This will help them predict what the character might do and say. This will also help them invent their own characters.

Ask the children why they thought they were doing the tasks. Compare their comments with your list. Do they relate to each other?

Discussion with mentors in school

- Observe and discuss the strategies used to help children understand the underpinning concepts and skills involved in their tasks. Give attention to the beginning, middle and plenary part of the lesson – were the strategies used equally explicit for every stage? Were the children clear about what they were trying to learn and why it was important?
- Discuss possible further tasks that could help develop these concepts and skills (possibly in another context).

Discussion on college-based courses

- Key concepts and skills in English and how they relate to other concepts and skills: Why are they important? What will they help children to be able to do?
- The importance of purpose for both teacher and pupils.
- The importance of 'authentic activities' where learning can be transferred.

References

Bruner, J. (1996) *Towards a Theory of Instruction*, Cambridge MA: Harvard University Press.

Clayden, E., Desforges, C., Mills, C. and Rawson, W. (1994) 'Authentic activity and learning', *Journal of Educational Studies* 42 (2) 163–73.

Hutchins, P.L. (1973) *Rosie's Walk*, London: Picture Puffins.

McKee, D. (1989) *Elmer*, London: Anderson Press.

Tochon, F. and Munby, H. (1993) 'Novice and expert teachers time epistemology: a wave function from didactic to pedagogy', *Teaching and Teacher Education* 9(2): 205–13.

Wood, D. (1988) *How Children Think and Learn*, Oxford: Blackwell.

10 Mathematics

Can trainees count?

Robin Foster

The unique place of mathematics

Mention mathematics to most people and you get an emotional response. Adults willingly confess that they can't do maths. They tell you how hard it was at school and how particularly heinous teachers tried to implant mathematics into their brains. Jokes about school mathematics unite generations of school children and adults in a shared culture of intrigues, mystery and fear, so any contemporary study of children's perceptions of their learning should attempt to address their reactions to school mathematics.

Several terms have been used in different contexts for what we now call school mathematics. Earlier in the century arithmetic tended to dominate. In most primary schools there was only arithmetic. Recently the terms 'numeracy' and 'number' have been used for school work related to computation and the manipulation of quantities. This is reflected in the phrase Numeracy Hour. The term numeracy emphasizes the importance of arithmetic – seen as the essential skills for a child to be competent in the mathematical basics. The actual implementation of the Numeracy Hour does however contain a wider experience of mathematics than mere arithmetical computations.

The inquiry reported in the chapter was carried out with Year 4 children. We were trying to find out how the children perceived mathematics when taught by trainees.

A reflective assessment of how subtraction has been taught

Changes in mathematics teaching over the past fifty or so years have been eloquently described in a beautiful essay by Gaea Leinhardt (1988). In a largely autobiographical account, she investigates the problems of teaching the basics of mathematics. She describes four different events. In the first, a bright young girl is being taught subtraction in a classroom in the late 1940s. The second takes place some twenty years later: Gaea is training to be an elementary teacher. A few years later she is teaching subtraction to primary-school children. The fourth event, in 1984, finds Gaea, now a researcher, interviewing children about subtraction and regrouping.

In the 1940s the children traded dimes and cents. In the 1950s and 1960s quite complicated explanations and definitions were given to student teachers. In a retrospective critique of the assigned textbook, Gaea says:

> Note that there is absolutely nothing in the text about how to teach. There is no reference to the student at all or what might be hard or easy to learn. There is a brief verbal mapping that indicates how each definition solves a different word problem. The mathematics is elegant and powerful. The pedagogy is lousy.

Her conclusion – 'The mathematics is elegant and powerful. The pedagogy is lousy' – is an indictment not only of the textbook but of the inevitable confusion for the children.

In the 1980s referents like Dienes base ten were used in a way similar to the dimes and cents of the 1940s. Gaea stresses not only the aspects of mapping, but also connections to the children's specific experiences. In transforming the pedagogy, it is necessary to recognize the learners and their problems as individuals, rather than as programmable calculators.

Gaea Leinhardt has brilliantly contextualized the changes in mathematics pedagogy, educational fads and research issues.

The context

Children from two Year 4 classes in Clappersgate Primary, a large primary school in a market town in Cumbria, are at the centre of our work. Year 4A is taught by Mrs Ferguson, the deputy head, and Year 4B by Mr Carpenter. For work in mathematics and literacy they are taught in ability groups and some children move to another classroom. Mrs Bird is a supply teacher who regularly substitutes in Year 4A. Mr Carpenter taught the higher ability mathematics group and Mrs Ferguson the other group. When the children were interviewed they were selected by the teachers from the mathematics groups.

A local college of further education arranges student placements in Clappersgate. During the period of our study one of their students, Martin Carrick, worked with computers in the classroom. He set up the computer and arranged support for the children as directed by the teachers.

St Martin's uses Clappersgate in a variety of its programmes. Trainees from the PGCE course are placed in the two Year 4 classrooms. At the beginning of the academic year, four students spend some time in each of the classrooms. They work in pairs for a period of a couple of weeks. They work with groups of children concentrating on core curriculum work as directed by the school and the college. Thus children could come into contact with a surprising number of adults who in various degrees are involved in the teaching process.

The next major input from trainees is in the second term, when two are placed on teaching practice in the two classrooms. In Mrs Ferguson's class the trainee was Ms Andrews and in Mr Carpenter's classroom it was Ms Sanderson.

Asking the questions

It was during this second term that children were interviewed. I spent time observing the trainee teachers in the classroom and during two days undertook interviews with individual children in the classroom while the regular schoolwork was going on. The children seemed relaxed and I took notes as they talked. All of the children knew me as I'm a regular visitor to the school and I occasionally work with whole classes on numeracy.

I wanted to try to find out some specific information. I asked them which area of mathematics they were good at, and what mathematics they had covered with the trainee teachers. Could they remember which trainee teachers they had been taught by? I asked about trainee teachers in general to give them an opportunity for general comments about trainee teachers, and to perhaps indicate if they had been taught by one. Eight children from Mrs Ferguson's class were interviewed and six from Mr Carpenter's class.

The asking of the questions was fairly relaxed and informal, but the specific areas of questions used were:

What is your name?
What is your teacher's name?
What maths are you good at?
What other teachers have taught you during this year?
What maths did they do with you?
What is a student or trainee teacher?

Method of selecting children

To a large extent the sample could be described as opportunist: my presence in the school was largely for other reasons. I worked with the teachers and students on an in-service course and as link tutor between the Clappersgate School and St Martin's College. I did suggest that the teachers choose children who represented a range of ability.

Discussion

My first observation is the remarkable amount of material the children were able to remember. The names of all of the adults appear with a great deal of accuracy. Not all children remembered all of the names, but all of the names were represented in the responses. The children were absolutely clear about who their own class teacher was. They also knew the name of the trainee who was currently in the classroom.

One piece of information from the data might offer an interesting social insight on into some aspects of classroom interaction. Martin Carrick, the student from the college of further education, was always referred to as Martin by one of the children but as Martin Carrick by another. Teachers and student teachers are referred to consistently by title and surname. This seems to suggest that the trainees are accepted as very much part of the teaching staff.

The children's specific perceptions of mathematics

The responses to the two questions about mathematics were illustrative. One unexpected response was that the children were quite natural about their description of the mathematics. None expressed any distaste or apparent fear about the subject. A muted expectation of the first question, however, was to see if they could identify areas within the curriculum which would be readily identified as mathematics. Two of the children were not sure. The other twelve responses were overwhelming mathematical. The content they described could be titled 'The Basics'. All were number based. The dominance of counting and work on number operations indicated that the children had a clear notion of what should and did happen in a mathematics lesson: it was something to do with working out things with numbers or counting. Multiplication tables were frequently mentioned. They were responding to a question which asked them to say what they were good at. Not only could they identify mathematical topic areas, but they felt comfortable in saying that they were quite good at material which was clearly central to arithmetic and mathematics.

The second mathematical area to be investigated was that of content taught by trainees. In asking the question about 'other teachers' the children were not prompted to make the connection with trainees. They were clear who their regular classroom teachers were. In some cases the regular supply teacher, Mrs Bird, was identified as one of the individuals in the list. This seems to indicate that some of the children made no distinction between the trainee teacher and any other teachers who worked in the classroom. Again the topic areas were remembered well and all of the children gave responses which indicated that the topics covered were indeed mathematical. It might be inferred from the responses that some of the work was construed as being different or unusual:

> Halves and quarters. Mr Turner and Mr Huxley showed us how to do a pop-up Christmas card.

With Ms Sanderson and Ms Jolly: Hundred Squares, Odds and Evens, Time tables.

Some trainees were obviously seen as people who offered sympathetic help:

When you are stuck he doesn't tell you the answer. He just explains it and then you get the answer.

On the other hand some of the responses indicated that some of the work with trainees reflected the popular view of mathematics:

How to work out sums.

How to do counting and maths. Mental tests!

The cumulative picture is a consistent one. The trainees are clearly identified as individuals who are seen as 'other teachers' in the classroom and the children are able to identify specific mathematics which they had been taught.

What is a trainee teacher?

The final question asked was about trainee teachers, and I used that term. Eight of the fourteen children said that they did not know what a trainee teacher was. This is particularly surprising since student teachers have been working in the classrooms throughout the year. It may be a particular tribute to the professional nature of the permanent teachers in the school that they are able to introduce and sustain work with trainee teachers in such a way that the children are not aware that the teacher who is teaching them is learning the job. It might also be that the children are particularly accepting of the various experiences. The fact that so many could not tell the difference between students and staff makes their responses more powerful. They were giving responses which were particular to the individuals who had taught them, rather than to abstract categories of 'trainee teacher', 'supply teacher' and their own 'classroom teacher'.

It is also at this point that the responses become general; none was specifically about mathematics. This might be expected as the trainees actually taught a variety of subjects and the nature of the question was general. It also indicates that for many children, even though they can identify individual subjects, the overall social experience of the classroom and learning is more all-embracing for them.

The children who did offer an opinion about 'trainee teachers' made interesting comments. Fraser thought that the further education student, Martin Carrick, was a trainee:

Like Mr Martin.

Some children seemed to know what a trainee was, but did not seem to see them as being particularly different from other teachers. Some work appeared to be done in ways which the children considered to be repeating previously covered material:

They are training to be a teacher. They are not really different.

They do different things, Go over things from last year. They help you if you don't know.

Other children commented on some aspects of the trainees' presence or way of working:

Like Ms Sanderson. Training to be teachers. They don't stay forever, only stay for weeks or months.

Someone training to be a teacher. Sometimes they work us hard and some times it is very easy.

The most perceptive comment came from Sally, who put her finger on a problem experienced by many children. In any classroom there are routines and ground rules set by the class-teacher and adhered to. A perennial problem for class-teachers taking back a class is how to re-establish this class culture – 'how we do things here'. Handwriting and the recording of things in a particular manner are two. Sally offers an observation which stresses how it might be true that the children's attention to the detail in handwriting might be closer than that of trainees. There must be a multitude of similar procedures which go unaddressed when a trainee is in charge of any class. But although the readjustment process is difficult, the children are endlessly accommodating and resilient.

It's a trainee teacher 'cos they're learning. Some times you have to correct them. Handwriting, you have to tell them how we do it here.

Conclusion

The inquiry indicates that children have a clear idea of the content of their learning, but when it comes to knowing about who it is that they are taught by, there is a degree of vagueness. However, the depth of their perceptions about the adults who come and go is evident in their responses.

Their comments show that they are deep-thinking individuals who take their learning seriously. Their opinions deserve to be taken seriously. It has to be remembered that the inquiry took place in a school which has a constant stream of student teachers. The children were actively involved in their learning and to an extent blissfully unaware of the additional demands that training teachers placed on their classroom. This should suggest to trainee teachers, teacher trainers and others responsible for the multi-faceted operations going on in the classroom that great care is needed when they try to meet their own targets. Perhaps they should recall that the real reason for the classroom is for the children themselves and *their* learning. This represents an awesome task, which is more important than anything else.

Suggestions for:

Further Reading

Foster, R. (1996) 'James and the giant procept', *Mathematics Teaching* 157, December pp. 5–7.
Merttens, R. (1997) *Teaching Numeracy: Maths in the Primary Classroom*, London: Scholastic.

Further investigations

In school look for opportunities to observe the children's mathematics learning. Make a collection of errors and misconceptions which you note as you work with the children. This might include examples from written work or by making notes of verbal material.

Discussion on college-based courses

- Compare your findings with other trainees, support workers and teachers. Are there any common features in the ways children demonstrate methods of working?
- Compare the outcomes of your work with the errors and misconceptions noted in Circular 4/98 *Teaching: High Status, High Standards*, (DfEE, 1998).
- What strategies can you use to help children develop their mathematical thinking?

References

Leinhardt G. (1988) 'Situated knowledge and expertise in teaching', in J. Calderhead (ed.) *Teachers' Professional Learning*, London: Falmer Press.

Part IV

New faces, new ideas?

11 Art and design
A view from the classroom

Jill Pemberton

The purpose of art is to close the gap between you and everything that is not you and thus proceed from feeling to meaning.

(Hughes 1982)

Illumination

As I eagerly reread the transcripts of the wonderful and often bizarre conversations with the children I recently interviewed in preparing for this chapter I recalled that, as a child, not many people asked my opinion about anything. In fact I don't think I was given much credit for having an opinion, let alone expressing it. Much later I realized that there was a time when assimilated preconception and conditioned response formed the major part of what I believed in and my philosophy on art, society and life in general was borrowed. I remember at times being quite passionate about these borrowed beliefs. At least I believed in something. And then the people who believed in me taught me, in a gentle and non-judgemental way, how to use the understanding I would gain as I made my art, how to recognize the rare instances of illumination which would mould those misconceptions, how to contour the conditioning and replace the purloined paradigms with a personal philosophy – tempered with a healthy dose of anarchism. By now it was my own epiphany. As I reflected on the changes which I have undergone – from quietly confident child to deeply doubting student; from professional painter to teacher and lecturer – I came to realize how important it is to remember that it takes time to develop beliefs and even longer to master the skills to share those beliefs.

I chose to begin this chapter with a quote from Robert Hughes because it made me acutely aware of one of the myths, which most new primary trainee teachers bring with them to the subject study of art and, in the case of most non-specialist trainees, to the act of *making* art: that it is a mainly non-cerebral and highly emotive activity, a purely expressive release.

Responses from potential trainees on interview, hoping to enter a four-year BA (QTS) course, to the question, 'How and what do you think children learn, through making and experiencing art?' illustrate this. The responses will inevitably include statements ranging from: 'Children can access ways to express themselves in art.'; or 'Children enjoy art – it's therapeutic'; or 'Children learn to *observe* carefully'; to 'Children who are *failing* in academic subjects often do well in art'.

There is little difference in the answers from potential art specialists and non-specialist interviewees. The changes in perception that trainees undergo over four years and the appreciation of this development which is reflected in the responses of the young students they teach are the substance of this chapter.

There are significant differences between the teaching approaches, attitudes and depth of subject knowledge of specialist and non-specialist trainees. The main reasons for these differences are rooted in the strengths of developed practice and the personal investment in their own creative growth, which specialist trainees develop during ITT. In this chapter, I look at examples of observed good practice which I hope trainee teachers will be encouraged to emulate and use as a guide in developing and evaluating their own approaches.

Art history?

The 1982 Gulbenkian report *The Arts in Schools* identifies 'restricted access to good arts practice as children' as being the main reason that primary teachers themselves are less prepared for the planning and teaching of a sound arts curriculum.

The pre-National Curriculum status of art (and the expressive arts in general) was lower than traditionally accepted academic subjects – maths, science, English – and tended to be regarded as an optional activity, largely limited to leisure time. Subsequently less time, fewer resources and less in-service training were devoted to art.

The majority of 1980s primary teachers also possessed a notion of artistic talent – that children have an inborn trait, an absolute quality – 'you've either got it or you haven't' – therefore rationalizing the fact that many children were not given the opportunity to engage with the joys, satisfaction and challenges of communication through art. That all children can learn within and through art is a difficult belief to nurture in trainees if they have this conditioned preconception that only a talented few will ever really achieve in this subject. If the trainees themselves have not experienced any art-making during the GCSE and A-level years, they will have no confidence in their own artistic abilities.

It is easy to see why the relationship between trainees and children can easily become tangled in threads of misunderstanding. Breaking those threads entails the removal of confusion in the mind of both trainee-teachers and pupils as to the intentions of the learning, the reasons for teaching the subject.

The trainee's initial misconceptions regarding their approaches to teaching art will only change through direct involvement in their own creative development. Only by experiencing the process of making art ourselves can we understand and convey to others the nature and power of that process.

In order to suggest strategies for trainees' own investigations into the effectiveness of their teaching, I needed to find out about the knowledge, attitudes, and beliefs of the children. If you want to know what children think they are learning and how they feel about it, ask them. This was yet another excuse to indulge myself in 'talking art' with children and to record some wonderful and revealing responses. My analysis of the children's responses will, I believe, help trainees question their own approaches to art teaching and to clarify both their teaching aims and their professional development needs.

'Why before how'?

Questioning children about their work is a valuable strategy for assessment (both while they are working and when the work is completed) but more beneficially, it can engender learning.

Take the word 'Why?'. It is one of the most frequently used words in the vocabulary of very small children (ask any harassed and exasperated parent). 'Why does it work?' 'Why did you do that?' 'Why can't I do this?' 'Why is the dog doing that?' 'Why do we die?'

The inquiring mind – the mind of a young child, desires reasons and the 'Why?' word strips away pretentiousness and asks us to confront the *purpose of doing*. This is occasionally an uncomfortable situation to be in. As teachers or potential teachers, we find it difficult to answer, 'I don't know why!'. What we need to learn is the way to turn the 'why?' question around and be confident enough in our ability to support inquiry and say, ' What do *you* think is the reason why?'.

Newland and Rubens (1989) quote Delia Smith (1981), 'There was a basic need for a cook book that told you not only how but why – why you mustn't add the egg quickly so it doesn't curdle/Why mustn't you overbeat the egg-whites?' to demonstrate their belief that the exploration of process in depth is fundamental to building confidence in the learner. I would add that encouraging self-questioning is the absolute basis for developing research skills and independent learning in a child.

So, how will my questions help you, as a student teacher, to encourage these desirable learning attributes?

It is back to untangling those threads of misunderstanding, of establishing in the minds of the pupils the reasons for the task. If children know why they are exploring a process it builds into the task an element of self evaluation – purposeful reflective learning. Children then naturally formulate the question 'What if . . .?'. Suddenly you are in a class filled with researchers and a possibility of thirty-two epiphanies. . . .

All art-making is research in the sense that it asks, 'what if . . .? of its materials or context (and conversely that making which is not research is not art)' (Waters 1994).

The visits – a walk on the wild side

My inquiry centred on three trainees all in their fourth-year, Final Block Placements at three primary schools; Kirkstone, St Joseph's and Manor Way.

Susan Dale with twenty-four Reception and Year 1 children. Susan's lesson within a Scheme of Work focused on a class visit to Grizedale Sculpture Park in Cumbria. The children then constructed assemblages on the school playing fields using found materials.

David Brown with twenty Year 6 children. David brought into class a contemporary piece of sculpture/assemblage as a focus for the children's work on Identity. They planned their own work using collage and relevant personal material.

Fiona Channing with sixteen Reception/Year 1/2 children. Fiona used the work of Miro to teach a lesson around the exploration of line using a variety of media, including computer graphics.

Simon Waters (1994) describes information as 'any difference that makes a difference . . .'. I collected my potential differences as I sat in on lessons and talked to the children.

'Data might be regarded as "dead" information which hasn't yet made a difference. When data becomes useful it becomes information' (ibid. 1994).

I gathered 'data' over a period of three months as I:

1   Questioned Susan, David and Fiona using pro-forma sheets.
2   Questioned children directly with pro-forma prompts during and after the observations.
3   Observed the trainees teaching art lessons.
4   Looked at lesson plans and made my own evaluations of their teaching.
5   Analysed photographs of children and their work.

My first visit was to Susan with her group of twenty-four Reception and Year 1 children. She had planned a comprehensive Scheme of Work around a visit to Grizedale Sculpture Park in Cumbria looking at the elements of line, form and texture in 3-D construction/assemblage. Susan consistently challenged children's ideas about making art with found, natural materials. The design process – planning, modifying, reviewing – was central but flexible and the constant conversation of questioning, prompting and directing ensured that the process (the art making), recorded on digital camera, took precedence over the end product. The class had also formed links with a large urban primary school so that the children could compare perspectives on the visit. The two classes exchanged photographs, poems and drawings of their work to encourage further discussion and analysis. I observed the class out on the school playing fields making pieces using found natural materials – sticks, stones, moss, twine, grasses, nuts, leaves. Susan had been teaching a science topic on water during the previous week and the children linked their understanding of water to their art work. They worked in small groups of four or five. As I walked around I asked questions. The children's replies were exciting, the 'art' language appropriate and accurate; the children demonstrated deep involvement in their research and analysis of process.

LOUISE: We are making sculptures about weather. Mine's a rain cloud.

THOMAS: It's not a sculpture it's an assemblage.

LOUISE: We are making things with sticks and moss and stones. I am tying stones on because I like the way they hang. I am choosing smooth stones. They are like raindrops.

DANIEL: The teacher tells us about artists in Grizedale and we like their work. We looked all day at Grizedale I made a drawing of a giant.

EMMA: This is an umbrella. I'm bending the stick. You have to look at it this way. It's from underneath. I want it this way. It's better like this. Look stand back here. It's better now. I'm choosing different things to put in each bit. I will put moss here.

OWAIN: We are choosing materials to make our sculpture from natural things, like they do at Grizedale. Sometimes they nail them together.

KATIE: I don't know if it will be finished. It might wash away in the rain.

JENNY: I asked Miss Dale about a sculpture and she told me how it was made. One day I will make a really big sculpture like Sally Mathews [a Grizedale artist]. I will make a dragon.

THOMAS: We made plans in the classroom first and then models. They're called maquettes. But it's ok to change as you make them if it is going better than your plan.

DAISY: I love doing this art. I didn't know this was art at first.

David Brown used a piece of work entitled *Identity* as a four-week focus with his group of Year 6 children. The children first talked about what 'elements' they could identify in the piece. They found examples of line, shape, space and texture and spent time looking at the piece with a magnifying glass. In groups they had been asked to brainstorm the word 'identity'. They were allowed to use dictionaries and a thesaurus. Here are some of the words and phrases they came up with:

who am I? describe me name recognize someone evidence
yourself find out belief proof place I live personal belongings
likes/dislikes family finger print revealed birth certificate

They then had to plan an assemblage using personal artefacts, photo-copies of evidence, personal preferences, etc. and begin the making. David asked them to use techniques that they had used in previous work such as basic collage and plaster bandage. Their responses to my questions included:

GARETH: I get really good ideas with Mr Brown. He talks softly and explains everything clearly.

JAMES: He doesn't have to get mad with us because we like the lessons he teaches.

ALICE: He thinks I am doing interesting work. My sketchbook is nearly full. Here's some postcards of Kurt Schwitters. He made collages like our work. I am going to put my ideas in little boxes.

SARAH: Mrs Norman (class-teacher) is going to put our work into an exhibition in town.

STUART: Me and Gary are working together and we are going to make a mystery piece. It will be very big and bright.

GARETH: Yeh loads of red 'cos we like Man U. [football team] we are going to make a big card trophy like the FA cup and put our bits in that.

CHARLOTTE: I am bringing in my holiday pictures and some photos of my great-great grandpa 'cos that's about me too.

ALICE: I want to photocopy my handprint and use it.

TOM: I found out about artists who make collage and assemblage. It's French. It means collecting and putting bits together. Sometimes paper. Sometimes building it up. You can use anything – junk, tickets, letters, and sometimes they look really naff, like unfinished, but they are interesting.

GARETH: It [the focus piece, *Identity*] looks like it is falling apart.

DAVID BROWN: Does that matter?

GARETH: Yes. If it's art it's supposed to last like that one in Paris that we looked at on *Eyewitness* [computer program] the *Mona Lisa* – that's dead old.

DAVID BROWN: Why must it last?

I was deeply impressed with David's planning which had reflected and built upon the children's culture. Good art-making draws upon percep-tions of context and an awareness of environment and change. It makes learning real. David was himself an artist. He used his own creative devel-opment as an energizing force in his professional teaching. His learning objectives reflected his understanding of open-ended process, but he had very high expectations of the children.

Fiona Channing was on the second week of a Scheme of Work around Line with her Reception, Year 1 and Year 2 children. She had planned to explore print, clay, drawing and painting with them. She had reproductions of several western and non-western artists to reinforce her teaching points.

When I arrived the children were gathered on the mat looking at a poster size reproduction of Miro's *Birds And Insects*. Fiona, in a very quiet voice, asked what they could see. Each child was invited to be involved in this exploration of lines, colours shapes and allegory. The children described the lines using an appropriate vocabulary. In four groups, they worked in rotation exploring lines with a variety of media including Paint, and a computer program. Joanne, a nursery nurse, worked at one table, while Fiona moved around the groups asking children to describe what marks they had made and how they used the tools. Then the children came back together to look at their work. I moved around the room asking questions as the children worked.

GEORGE: This is a thin line. If I turn the charcoal stick on its side it makes a fat line.

ALISTAIR: My lines make a pattern because they go in the same way.

SIOBAHN: Miro is funny. Miss Channing says his pictures make her sing.

PETER: His pictures jump around [begins to bang pencil on paper] like this. See, jumpy marks!

GRAHAM: I think that bit is like a jelly fish with tentacles.

VICTORIA: No it's the feathers of a bird's wing. You can read a title which sometimes tells you things about the picture. This one is called *Flying* I think, so it's probably about birds.

SAM: The picture isn't like real but it can look like birds.

REBECCA: It's fun working with lines on the computer. Look at this one – it's a big slug.

DAVID: No it it's a man's leg!

SAM: Miss Channing says that I can take my line for a walk.

ANNA: Sometimes Miss Channing stops us and makes us tell her what we know about lines and things. I know loads. I didn't. Do you want to see my sketch book?

ME: Yes please!!

Then I embarked on the second stage of my inquiry: to analyse my data within the three frameworks of the Standards set out in the DfEE Circular 4/98:7–15.

Standard A: knowledge and understanding

This was clearly evident in the teaching of all three students and was reflected in the confidence and enthusiasm of their teaching, in the stretching questions they asked and in their responses to the children's inquiries about technique, process and content. Their strong subject knowledge was evident in the 'overviews' of sequential experience they planned and implemented and their awareness of the stages of development in making art. Their teaching of research skills through and within art learning was evident in the reflective analysis which the children demonstrated in their sketchbooks and used in their integrated approach, demonstrating their knowledge and understanding through recording their observations, gathering resources and materials to develop their ideas in different media, and reviewing their work as it progressed.

Standard B: planning, teaching and class management

Planning for the individual art lessons was fixed within Schemes of Work. The understanding that art cannot be taught meaningfully as an isolated lesson was evident. Expectations for children's learning and involvement were high. The students' confidence in secure subject knowledge was reflected in their teaching approaches, enabling them to stimulate intellectual curiosity and generate enthusiasm in the lessons. The awareness of creative and cognitive developmental stages, brought about by a reflective and analytical approach to their *own* progression within a rigorous art degree course, enabled them to match tasks and teaching methods appropriately.

Susan, David and Fiona demonstrated an awareness, in both planning and teaching, that good art-making draws upon children's perceptions of their own cultural contexts; the students used this in creative and effective ways. Fiona Channing took eloquent, penetrating risks in the discussion of Miro's work which enthralled the pupils and rewarded her with examples of acute observations, framed in a mature art vocabulary, from her Year 1 and Year 2 children. Organization and management of the lessons reflected a familiarity and confidence in the media and realistic expectations of what could be accomplished in the allotted time. All trainees had detailed evaluations reflecting on the learning objectives for the whole scheme and individual lessons. They used this new found knowledge to amend and expound future lessons.

Standard C: monitoring, assessment, recording, reporting and accountability

Susan, David and Fiona demonstrated a variety of assessment methods, including encouraging children to record the stages of their art-making with pictures and words in sketchbooks. They used this evidence and the completed work to evaluate to what extent children had achieved predetermined criteria within the Programme of Study for Art. Assessment was built into the best planning in the form of questions and interventions. They encouraged the children to become involved in identifying ways to develop and improve their work. One group of children was encouraged to reflect on previous work undertaken with the trainee and assess their own progress. The quality of the conversations maintained throughout the lessons reflected the trainees' understanding of the importance of giving pupils the ability and confidence to move towards ownership of their learning through fluency of visual language. At the end of lessons each of the students had gathered their class together to discuss the work they had been doing. There were valuable, structured opportunities for reflective evaluation of their learning.

Summary

The original question this book looks at is whether or not trainee teachers are *good* for children. My findings would suggest that they *can be*.

The best of the lessons observed contained the following definable attributes, specifically related to the teaching and learning of art:

1   They were planned within a Scheme of Work, based on an understanding of children's creative and cognitive development and building upon *sequence, continuity* and *progression*.
2   They demonstrated a working knowledge of the materials, skills and techniques needed to ensure involvement, enjoyment and success in the process.
3   They reflected, in their breadth of possibility and open-ended approach, an awareness that a curriculum in art integrates both specific and generic skills, provides a fertile ground for investigation and is constantly redefining and discovering itself.
4   They were aware of contextual relationships to the world outside, encouraging this awareness in the children they worked with. The content of the lessons planned within that framework was constructed on broad and culturally differentiated fronts.
5   They reflected a scepticism of token integration of art with either other arts subjects or other curriculum areas for the sake of addressing recent 'breadth and balance' directives. Integration comes from the Latin *integrare* which means 'to make whole'. The danger is, that often making whole of several areas of conceptual understanding can trivialize and promote superficiality.
6   They all made use of language to expand the clarity and poignancy of the children's visual experiences 'Perception helps talking and talking fixes the grains of perception' Gibson (1965). The language was accurate and reflected a knowledge and understanding of the concept.
7   They all had high expectations of their pupils. They attacked the barrier of talent with a comprehension of the value of art education for all. 'Art remains one of the few non-goal oriented areas of human activity in a functionalist world' (Waters 1994).

Discussion with mentors in school

- Can mentors use the questions to help students teach art more effectively?
- Are students able to identify areas of strength and weakness in their art teaching and learning?
- Should these be identified in profiles for further development?

Discussion on college-based courses

- Can we improve the subject knowledge and practical understanding of non-specialist trainees within the present constraints on allotted contact time prescribed in the current validated courses?
- Do mentors require in-service provision to improve their knowledge base as part of mentor training?
- Can trainees work more closely (trailing, in-school training) with subject specialists in school-based practice?
- Are we providing enough quality professional development training for mentors and NQTS?

References

Calouste Gulbenkian Foundation (1982) *The Arts in Schools: Principles, Practice and Provision*, London: Calouste Gulbenkian Foundation.

DfEE (1998) Circular 4/98, *Teaching: High Status, High Standards*, Teacher Training Agency.

Gibson, J. (1965) *The Senses Considered as Perceptual Systems*, London: Greenwood Press.

Hughes, R. (1982) *The Shock of the New*, London: Thames and Hudson

Newland, M. and Rubens, M. (1989) *A Tool for Learning: Some Functions of Art in Primary Education*, London: Calouste Gulbenkian Foundation.

Smith, D. (1981) *The Other Hunger*, in Newland and Rubens (1989).

Waters, S. (1994) *Living Without Boundaries*, Bath: Bath College of Higher Education Press.

12 Music as you like it?

Kevin Hamel

It is clear that ways into entitlement for music may extend beyond what is currently practised in many schools. There are new skills to be learned as music and ICT draw closer together and become ever-more sophisticated. Musical opportunities are opening up and new ways of doing things are emerging through ICT. Students often have good ICT skills and this can be a useful way in for students, children and teachers to evolve a genuine partnership in teaching music.

Since all student teachers must achieve a prescribed level of skills in ICT their increasing levels of confidence and expertise bring new possibilities in integrated learning in the arts. There are areas of children's musical experience that trainees can take a lead in promoting.

The *Guidance in Music: A Pupil's Entitlement to ICT* (NCET/Ofsted 1996) publication which was circulated to all primary schools, suggested three important ways in which ICT could contribute to the enhancement of pupils' perceptions, experiences and musical skills:

1   Using and investigating sounds and structures.
2   Refining and enhancing performance and composition.
3   Extending knowledge of different styles of music.

Before a group of student teachers began their teaching practice, I asked the pupils, whose classrooms they would be working in, about their expectations of lessons in a number of foundation subjects. Their expectations were clearly influenced by their experiences of previous trainees. Children had responded enthusiastically to a history trip to York in connection with work on the Vikings. They had been given opportunities to examine evidence from a dig, and speculated on the possibility of similar work on another such trip. Others had enjoyed imaginative lessons in dance and PE based on Maurice Sendak's picture book *Where the Wild Things Are* and hoped that the 'new' teachers would be planning similar experiences.

When pupils were questioned about music, their responses were less positive. They seemed to expect that even if student teachers were involved, music lessons would be 'more of the same'. Comments from Year 4 children included:

> You listen to the tape, then you sing with it. Sometimes the teacher'll choose some people to play some instruments while the rest of us sing.

> You play what you're told on the instruments. Usually the girls get the glockenspiels.

> We might make up our own music. I can play *Eastenders*.

> We'll listen to music and say if we like it. It was *Peter and the Wolf* last time.

> She'll expect us to sing. I won't sing though.

Although further discussion revealed that they had much more positive expectations of work in other subjects, their pessimism about music classes was evident. Why should this be?

Trainees themselves tend to feel insecure about their ability to teach music. Many have not enjoyed their own time in school music classes; many are unsure of their own musical ability and their competence to teach music. Music tutors recognize this and work hard to put student teachers at their ease and to make music accessible. However, such courses are brief, and may do little more than attempt to indicate the range and place of music in the curriculum, brush up on a few skills and suggest resources and avenues for help.

If there is a skilled music specialist working in the school, it may be daunting to pick up on the work. Trainees worry that children will compare their efforts unfavourably. Conversely, music may be a time when a well-meaning but ineffective parent or member of the community, who has volunteered solely because of their ability to play the piano, presides over poor behaviour as children 'try it on' during a music lesson.

The Gulbenkian report (1982) described 'ways of seeing' unique to the arts. The ICT multimedia revolution has opened up new possibilities. The National Curriculum orders for music make it clear that music has its own unique set of concepts to be developed, skills to be taught, and repertoire and history to be critically examined. Traditionally, this has been the province of the music specialist. However, new developments in ICT and music education open up new opportunities for trainees and non-specialist classroom teachers to plan and carry out the musical education.

Compose World Junior is a well-tried and easy-to-use program for music composition, first introduced for the BBC computer in the 1980s. It is regularly updated and is now available on Windows 95, Windows 3.1 and for Acorn RisCOS (requires 1 Mb RAM). It is designed to encourage musical listening and decision-making; even very young pupils find it simple and satisfying to use. It also poses challenges and suggests musical possibilities to quite advanced musicians.

Pupils can choose from a series of musical phrases represented pictorially, and compose their own melodies by 'dragging and dropping' the pictures on to a grid. Musical phrases can be arranged in varying combinations to create longer and balanced melodies. The process is akin to arranging and re-arranging musical 'building blocks'. *Unit 3B: Manipulating Sound* uses a similar program in the exemplar scheme of work for ICT.

To be able to manipulate pre-composed musical phrases in this way is extremely useful. Pupils can select from at least seventy different sets of pictures and phrases (tune files) representing a great variety of musical styles and traditions, and thus become familiar with musical structures and scales, and techniques such as imitation and variation. New tune files are constantly being added and are available through an associated Internet site and a range of web-based publications. They provide major, minor, whole-tone, pentatonic and chromatic scales, and musical styles such as Chinese, Appalachian, Near Eastern and Indian.

The program is not intended as a quick fix to address the entirety of the National Curriculum orders for music. Central to the process of music education is the notion of pupils composing their own music and performing it using voices and instruments. *Compose World Junior* is both a stimulus for these activities and a creative forum to enhance their musical

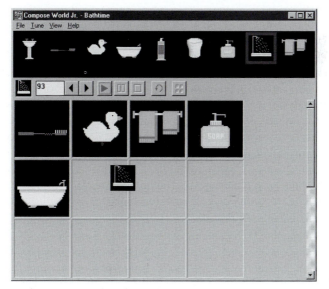

Fig 12.1 'Bathtime' screenshot from the *Compose World Junior* program.

listening. For example, pupils introduced to the pentatonic scale could learn to sing American pentatonic songs such as 'Eliza Jane'. Then using *Compose World Junior*, they could listen to phrases composed in an Appalachian folk style and use the pentatonic scale as a starting-point for composing their own pentatonic tunes and accompaniments to songs.

This involves an appraisal process: the children consider the musical choices they are making. They listen carefully to, and then discuss and compare, musical phrases before selecting and sequencing them to create a melody. The children can practise singing each of the phrases and consider which might be good beginnings or good endings.

Once a good beginning for a melody has been chosen, the user points to the picture, holds down the mouse button and drags it on to the first box of the grid (the sequencer). The picture appears in the box as the button is released. By using the video recorder-style controls underneath the pictures ('transport bar'), the music may be played, stopped, paused or constantly repeated ('looped').

There is a danger that younger pupils might be attracted by the notion of creating a repeating pattern of pictures or musical phrases which appeal to them. *Compose World Junior* guards against this by enabling the musical grid to be limited to just four spaces. In this way, rambling and musically incoherent sequences may be avoided. Pupils should be encouraged to listen critically to their completed melodies, and to replace phrases with others after considering their effect within the overall melody. Gradually, they will come to appreciate the structural possibilities of repeating phrases within longer melodies, and should be encouraged to strive for balance and to listen out for structures in the songs they sing.

The sinking of the *Titanic*: A case study

The work took place at St Guthlac's C.E. Primary School with Year 6 children. The junior department had one multimedia Pentium-based computer, recently connected to the Internet. The school was keen to promote the use of ICT and the Internet across curriculum areas, and a very able and enthusiastic teacher, Helena McCallum, acted as ICT co-ordinator to encourage and support colleagues. She knew about *Compose World Junior* from a previous school, where the pupils had used it independently, but she had not really thought about its potential.

Elizabeth Paxton was a final-year university student about to embark on a PGCE Primary course. She considered her ICT skills 'about average'. A requirement of the course was that she spend some time in a primary school before beginning her studies. She had seen *Compose World Junior* demonstrated during a module on music and education, and was keen to try it for herself. She was able to follow the on-screen instructions to install the program, and had become familiar with using the Internet during the module. Because she had enjoyed the James Cameron film *Titanic* (and had seen it three times!), she decided that it might make an inviting focus.

During preliminary discussion, it emerged that the children knew a lot of facts (and fiction!) about the sinking of the *Titanic*. Elizabeth showed them video footage of the actual deep-sea exploration of the wreck, with the idea that the children would create their own 'sound track' and musical documentary.

The ESP *Titanic* web site is a treasure store of musical examples, music activities and cross-curricular links centred on the *Titanic* disaster. Although the site is intended to be used in conjunction with *Compose World*, a number of the activities and ideas can be used without the program.

The story begins with the confused messages regarding the ship's fate following garbled Morse transmissions, resulting in the morning press reporting that all passengers were safe and that the damaged liner was being towed to port. Pupils are introduced to two musical activities based on rhythm: the first involves sending SOS messages using pitched chime bars, the second makes use of a musical Morse transmitter, which can be downloaded from the web.

Elizabeth arranged the children into groups of six, each with a chime bar. They practised making long and short sounds, discovered that they needed to stop the bar vibrating for short sounds, and evolved a range of techniques to achieve this. They were introduced to the notion of Morse code, and read a report from the *Daily Mirror* for Tuesday 16 April, stating that the *Titanic* was afloat and being towed to port with no loss of life. Elizabeth explained that the messages had become confused, because the ship's transmitters were not powerful enough to convey messages to shore without relaying them through other vessels equipped with Marconi transmitters. A game of 'Chinese whispers' demonstrated how messages become confused in a few moves. Back in their groups, they practised the SOS signal until everyone could do this confidently. Then each group arranged itself in order of players 1 to 6. Player 1 was the radio operator of the *Titanic*, and played the SOS message. This was played, or 'relayed' by player 2, as the imaginary radio operator of a ship in the vicinity, and passed on to player 3, etc. Performances were developed and refined by players continuing to play the distress signal, thus creating interesting rhythmic and melodic textures.

After listening to the performances, a 'musical' Morse transmitter was downloaded from the *Titanic* Internet site. This contained Morse signals for every letter of the alphabet, and children were able to put together the 'call' signs and messages from the *Titanic* by dragging the letters on to the grid and playing them as previously described.

In the video of the *Titanic* exploration, the remote camera zoomed in on the Marconi hut from which the SOS signals had been transmitted. Amazingly, much of the equipment seemed intact. In experimenting with chime bars, the children had discovered that an atmospheric undulating sound could be achieved by striking the chime bar, and rapidly and regularly stopping and releasing the sound hole with the thumb. They were fascinated by this vibrato effect and quickly became proficient at controlling the rate. One of the children suggested that this sounded like Morse code being played underwater!

Next, they consulted an on-line source, the *Encyclopaedia Titanica*, to find out about the ship's band and the music they played. On a web site dedicated to the pianist-composer, Scott Joplin, they listened to the ragtime music played as the passengers boarded the lifeboats. Using the *Compose* program, they were able to create their own ragtime pieces through combining phrases typical of the style.

Finally, they listened to and learned the words and music of 'Nearer My God to Thee', the hymn the band played, as the great liner descended to its watery graveyard.

The children loved their musical exploration of the *Titanic*, and the classroom teachers were genuinely surprised that ICT could contribute in such a wide-ranging fashion in music classes. Elizabeth brought expertise to and new perspectives on the teaching of music to the school.

> It was wicked! You can make really proper tunes which don't sound crap.

So often, children are disappointed with their musical results because of poor quality instruments and lack of technical expertise to help them achieve the musical results they want.

> I liked getting music off the computer and listening to it.

The Internet offers easy access to an infinite array of musical styles and traditions. Pupils can collect their own selection of music as part of a personal study and include clips to illustrate their written work.

> We never done music like this. I like choosing different sounds like piano and clarinet and seeing what they sound like playing the tune.

Children were interacting with the music, experimenting and discovering combinations of instruments, and developing valuable insights into principles of orchestration.

A Year 5 classroom teacher, Maria Ferrori, invited Elizabeth to help her with a musical dramatization of a Chinese folk tale *The Broken Lute String*. On a holiday in China Maria had seen a performance by the Peking Opera and wanted to encourage pupils to perform their own Chinese music. Elizabeth located a web site devoted to the Peking Opera, which included traditional stories and characters, and information and pictures of traditional costume and make-up. Using a Chinese musical file from *Compose World Junior*, the children were able to make up authentic melodies to accompany each character.

The applications of new technology to performance, composition, listening and appraising, and the need to make effective cross-curricular links if a broad and balanced curriculum is to be maintained calls into question the notion of a specialist able to advise staff on all aspects of music within the curriculum. Effective specialists have known for many years that the breadth and delivery of the music curriculum is a team effort, and welcome new perspectives from trainees and colleagues. Traditional musical skills are important, but trainees do not need personal instrumental skills in order to make substantial and effective contributions to children's musical learning. What is necessary is enthusiasm and the confidence to explore new avenues and possibilities.

Suggestions for:

Further reading

NCET/Ofsted (1996) *Music: A Pupil's Entitlement to ICT*, Coventry: SCAA Publications.
Myatt, A. and Paynter, J. (1991) *Sounding It Out*, Warrington: Dawsons.
Compose World Junior is available from: ESP Music, 21 Beech Lane, West Hallam, Ilkeston, Derbyshire DE7 6GP. http://www.espmusic.co.uk
A concessionary student pack is available to full-time trainees. It includes the *Compose World Junior* program for Windows 3.1/Windows 95, teachers' materials and a guide to Music and ICT at KS1 and KS2.

Further investigations

Discover resources available on the web. There are sites which directly relate to NC orders for music, and suggest a progressive range of activities. Other sites give access to a wide range of musical styles which can be saved to disc and replayed on the media player of Windows 95.

The following addresses are worth exploring:

- Dedicated music education sites:

  Children's Music Site http://cmw.cowboy.net/WebG
  This site provides access to a number of extremely useful sites including:
  Allegro – The Music Education Search Site http://talentz.com/Allegro.hts
  A wide ranging and logically organized site with an easy to use and effective search facility.
  Becta http://www.becta.org.uk
  Music and ICT in the curriculum

- MIDI sites:

  Classical Midi Archive http://www.prs.net/midi.html
  An outstanding collection of classical music in MIDI format which
  may be played on the Windows 95 media player.

Discussion with mentors in school

How do children respond to ICT applications in music? What evidence
is there of developing musical knowledge and skills? When is the use of
technology appropriate/inappropriate?

Discussion on college-based courses

How can teachers and trainees evolve effective partnerships, sharing
musical and ICT skills to explore new and effective ways of addressing
the NC orders for music?

References

Calouste Gulbenkian Foundation (1982) *The Arts in Schools: Principles, Practice
    and Provision*, London: Calouste Gulbenkian Foundation.
NCET/Ofsted (1996) *Music: A Pupil's Entitlement to ICT*, Coventry: SCAA
    Publications.
Sendak, M. (1967) *Where the Wild Things Are*, London: Bodley Head.

13 Information and communication technology

Who dares wins!

Liz Elliott and Pete Saunders

Thank you very much for your help

your welcome

Recent Ofsted reports (HMSO 1996/96, 1997/98) have noted that, generally, while good work in ICT was going on at Key Stage 1, Key Stage 2 children were underachieving. We decided to carry out an inquiry with Key Stage 2 children in four classrooms where trainee teachers on the four-year BA (QTS) programme were finishing their Final Block Placement before graduation. All of the trainees had successfully completed the ICT section of the Qualified Teacher Status examinations.

Our inquiry had three focuses. We wanted to find out first whether the children were confident in the trainees' knowledge about computers; second if the children felt that they were well-organized so that they had a chance to use computers effectively when working with student teachers; and third whether the children thought that computers were used to teach subjects across the curriculum. To overcome the possibility of 'compliant agreement', in designing our inquiry we devised both negative and positive statements. In this way, agreement with both 'We use computers everyday' and 'Most days we don't get to use the computers' would cancel each other out. We mixed the positive and negative statements randomly.

We followed the same routine in each of the four classes. First of all we emphasized that the survey was not a test, that it was completely anonymous and was in no way an evaluation of their (trainee) teacher. We gave each child a copy of the survey and went through a light-hearted training session with two sample questions written on the chalkboard. The children had time to ask questions and we showed them what to do if they changed their minds or decided not to respond to a particular question because they did not have a strong opinion either way. When we were sure that everyone knew the procedure, one of us read out the questions and the other helped children who weren't sure what to do. At the end of the survey we invited the children to write a sentence about their computer work, taking care to say that this was an option.

'Knowing about computers'

The first section of the survey aimed to find out to what extent children had confidence in their trainee teachers' personal computer skills and ability to help them to develop their own. The statements the children were asked to agree or disagree with and their responses are shown in Table 13.1. The analysis in Figure 13.1 shows that children strongly agreed with the positive statements about trainees' computer expertise and disagreed with the negative ones. They felt that trainees could 'help them when they were stuck' (A1), explain things clearly (A2) and set interesting tasks (A7). They did not think that the trainees were dependent on the class teachers' computer knowledge (A8). In fact they thought that the trainees used computers quite a lot in their own work (A9).

Most of the children were clear about what they were supposed to be doing when they were working with computers (A10); (half of those who were not were from the same class). They did not feel that expectations were unrealistic (A4) and they thought that their work with computers was expected to be of a high standard (A11). Overall there was a perception of the student teacher as someone who 'knows about computers'. We found tenacious loyalty to the trainee in all the classrooms we visited.

Table 13.1   Children's responses to statements which investigate their perceptions of trainees' knowledge about computers

Statements A	Disagree	Agree
When we work with Ms/Mr X he/she ...		
A1 can help you when you are stuck	0	96
A2 explains things clearly	2	90
A3 needs us to show him/her what to do	64	22
A4 gives us more complicated programs to use	83	12
A5 gives us work on the computer that we have already done	58	38
A6 says it's good work when it isn't	55	41
A7 sets challenging or interesting tasks	3	91
A8 has to keep asking our teacher how to ...	77	16
A9 uses the computer him/herself a quite lot	21	77
A10 doesn't realize that we are not sure what we are supposed to be doing	75	24
A11 expects high quality work	16	80

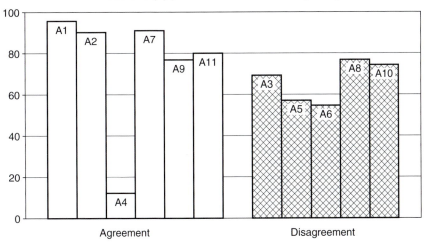

Scenario (A) (teacher 'knows about' computers)

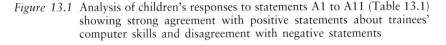

Figure 13.1 Analysis of children's responses to statements A1 to A11 (Table 13.1) showing strong agreement with positive statements about trainees' computer skills and disagreement with negative statements

Classroom management

Children's responses to statements concerned with trainees' classroom skills when organizing work with computers are shown in Table 13.2 and analysed in Figure 13.2. The children in the four participating classes were less positive about the trainee teachers' ability to manage the way computers were used than they were about their knowledge about computers. The main findings from this section of the survey were that most of the children agreed that the trainee always checked their work before they moved on (B6), and made sure that the equipment was working before they were sent to use it (B10). Very few of the children felt that they knew when it would be their turn to use a computer (B7), and many felt that access to the computers was unfair. However, it is important not to generalize from this small sample as some responses in this section were skewed by a situation in a particular class. Children's responses to the statements about the management of computer use in the classroom are shown in Table 13.2 and analysed in Figure 13.2.

Use of computers in subject areas

Children strongly supported the statement that Information Technology was an integrated part of the curriculum; they did not generally see the trainee teacher as someone who segregated computer work from routine classroom activities across the curriculum. More than 80 per cent said

> Mr constine is very Ceaver when it Comes to Computers.

Voluntary report

Besides the direct survey, the children were invited to add any comment they wanted to make but only if they had something they wanted to say.

Only a few children responded here. The comments received were heartening but it should be remembered that the responses were only from children identified by their willingness and ability to engage in an additional writing task. The comments fell into four main categories.

1   Children, both in the survey and their invited comments, see their trainee teachers as computer literate and computer confident.

Computers are very good with Miss Kendal. Miss Kendal has told us a lot about computers and I wish she could be here forever.

It is good having computers with Miss Stavely.

I like PCs and the work that Miss Stavely does on them.

When it comes to computers, Mr Hutton is clever.

His ICT lessons are brilliant.

2   Trainees are supportive and give help when needed.

Mr Hutton speaks clear and he is good on computers.

Miss Stavely tells us a lot about what we do.

Miss Kendal explains what we are doing and asks to double check we are sure.

3 The children feel that the trainees provided a range of computer usage, even taking into consideration problems of access to working equipment.

We cut and paste pictures

I like the digital camera

He lets us put on our names in different writing and it was really good.

In Miss Stavely's lessons on computers, we made company names, it was fun.

She teaches us about italics and fonts.

4 Fair access will always present difficulties but the children's comments reveal disappointment and patience.

I never got my turn and everybody else got a turn.

It's good in Mr Hutton's lessons but I haven't had a shot [a turn yet].

I have never been on the computer before but I would like to go on it.

We don't all get to use them in even two lessons.

We thought that you might like to see that we even got some personal feedback from our study in the classroom! An addition to our thank-you message on the bottom of the survey.

Thank you very much for your help

your welcome

appropriate and helpful; however, 35 per cent felt that they had too little time on the subject; 65 per cent felt they were underprepared to teach swimming. For many the teaching of gymnastics (38 per cent) and dance (32 per cent) was also problematic. Athletics and outdoor and adventurous activities caused little concern.

Trainees were asked about their general attitude to sport and fitness issues. Sixty-eight per cent enjoyed some kind of physical activity and valued the fitness benefits. The most popular activities were walking, exercise to music, and swimming, rather than participation in a specific sport. The most popular sports were netball, hockey and football. Twenty-three per cent did not undertake any physical activity at all.

Twenty-five of the survey students were selected for interviews balanced in terms of gender, age and subject specialism. PE specialists were not included since I could assume that they would have a high level of commitment to and competence in PE.

The interviews were revealing. One trainee admitted that she did not really like PE and had successfully avoided taking PE on her teaching practice throughout the four years! Her range of strategies to avoid PE including taking music instead, feigning injury and using the hall time for a drama production. The trainees had very little time to develop their own curriculum content and were for the most part reliant on the necessarily limited curriculum content and ideas given on their course. However, they felt that they had learned about the 'skill' and 'craft' of teaching PE on their teaching practice placements and appreciated the help they had received from teachers and mentors. However, this help was related to issues of timing, control and organization rather than curriculum content. It was also clear that several of the schools appreciated the new ideas that the student teachers demonstrated, and the class teachers saw them as part of their own professional development.

Concerns of trainees in teaching PE

Trainees approach PE teaching in different ways, based on their previous ability and experience. PE is an emotive subject, evoking past memories. For some, PE at school was a deeply embarrassing and humiliating experience. They have never been good at sport and were put into situations which highlighted their lack of co-ordination and ability. Other trainees have had more positive experiences of PE during their school days, but even they will have enjoyed a fairly limited number of sports. Many will have specialized in only one or two. David Kirk (1999) Professor of Youth Sport at Loughborough University, has found that several factors led to children's alienation from PE and sport. Adolescents, girls in particular, found the traditional curriculum based on team games unsuitable, because they resented structured or forced activities. Netball and cross-country running needed to be replaced by more focused activities, such as self-defence, dance, aerobics and alternative sports, such as football and softball. Schools need to allow pupils to wear warm, comfortable, up-to-date sportswear, rather than insisting on outdated PE kit.

Since there are six areas of activity in the NCPE most trainees will be asked to teach areas that they have little experience of. Teaching swimming looms as a horrendous undertaking for non-swimmers. The lack of time given to training in PE curriculum content may mean that the teacher training institutions are not able to provide enough instruction to counter these fears. The Ofsted report, *Teaching PE in the Primary School* (1998) notes that the hours for PGCE PE courses vary from 7.5 to 60 and for undergraduate PE courses from 7.5 to 90. The report states, 'The lower end of both ranges is clearly insufficient to enable trainees to learn how to teach all aspects of PE effectively'.

Susan Capel (1997) found that trainees have a wide range of concerns in the teaching of PE. These include organization and management of lessons; lesson delivery, including communication skills, discipline and class control; knowledge; planning and personal issues including lack of confidence and dislike of being observed.

Many of these concerns are generic, applicable in the teaching of any subject. However, the particular demands made by PE mean that they are especially evident. In this survey most anxiety seemed to be caused by perceived lack of knowledge and competencies. They are afraid that they don't know how to develop a theme or scheme. Officiating at unfamiliar sports can be a real trial, and it is not unknown for a trainee to ask the children about a particular rule.

What are the children's views of the teaching of PE by trainees?

This aspect of the study involved eighty-seven children in six different primary schools in north-west England. The schools ranged from a two-teacher rural school to a large urban school with over 350 pupils. The schools were asked to suggest children to be interviewed who had recent experience of being taught by trainee teachers. Thirty-four children were from Years 4 and 5; fifty-three were from Year 6. The interviews took place in the school; the class teacher was not present. The children's responses were taped and later transcribed. The format was that of a semi-structured interview with groups of three to four children. This allowed time for all the children to be asked the same questions, and also to ask further questions on particular points. My purpose was to evaluate pupils' perceptions of being taught PE by trainee teachers. I analysed the transcripts and then established five categories for discussion of the children's comments: differences from the class teacher; curriculum content; class control and behaviour; age factor; gender.

Children's perceptions of trainee teachers

Perceived differences from the class teacher

Children commented on the change of routines that trainees brought. Some children seemed to enjoy the unpredictability of lessons, other did not. This unpredictability was related to the curriculum content of the lesson and teaching style. One child said

> We never know what Miss Longman is going to do in PE.

This is perhaps inevitable, with trainees having to 'discover' the accepted routines. PE in particular is full of such routines: how the apparatus is set out and used; how the equipment is stored; how the children are expected to dress; and safety rules. Trainees may unknowingly add to the disturbance to routine by not fully explaining why the changes were made or why they were decided at short notice.

Other differences relate to content and the way the children were managed. Key phrases seem to be important to the children, as does the tone of voice.

> She never tells us what to do, she just expects us to know it.

> She always sounds angry.

There may be a case here for trainees to adopt certain approved characteristics of the class teacher, even if this is only for the duration of the placement.

One interesting perception was from a group of Year 6 children at St George's Junior School. They clearly appreciated the different status that they felt trainees accorded them.

> The students co-operated with you and were really nice.

> They [the trainees] didn't treat us like children. The teachers treat you like children. Do your work [mimic]. You just can't talk to them.

Another group of children at the same school made more negative observations about trainees, although not directly related to PE.

> The older teachers can spell better, sometimes the students can't spell, and the teachers know more stuff because they have been working for longer, so it's better to have your teacher for information.

Curriculum content

Children had a clear perception of receiving 'different' teaching experiences from trainees in terms of lesson content. Teachers do look to trainees as a source of new ideas, perhaps perceiving their own teaching as lacking in the latest developments in the area (Lavin 1999). However, the children were not necessarily fulsome with their praise for trainees. The use of the parachute in PE lessons was given as an example of what they enjoyed, although its 'newness' has now worn off somewhat.

Some children had a fairly sophisticated concept of the pace of the lessons and that they kept having to do the same movement experience repetitively.

> With Miss Sutton we just had to do forward rolls and then backward rolls and pencil rolls. Loads of rolls, every single roll ever invented and then you had to practise and practise.

This quote may reveal more about the lack of adequate training in gymnastics than the trainee's lack of expertise. As I have said many trainees will have had very limited time in training courses and this is reflected in the limited nature of the curriculum content they offer. The use of topics by trainees was discussed by one class and how it related to the content of their PE lessons.

> Once we did this poem about a highwayman, yeah we even had to do lots of lessons about it, even the PE was about it. It was boring, we had to do a poem, then a play, then PE, then a picture.

The children had many positive responses about the teaching of games by trainees. Many of them appreciated that it gave them a choice of activities. In two of the schools the trainee provided games options for Years 5 and 6. The children really enjoyed learning new games such as volleyball. Part of this success was due to the competence and confidence of the trainees, probably acquired by playing and coaching in their own schooldays.

Gymnastics and dance were not viewed in the same way by the children and they clearly felt their class teacher was the supervisor in teaching both these areas. Several children in one class spoke of the confusion they felt during a dance lesson they had with the trainee.

> First it was dance, then it was movement. She was running around, then she said side to side, and we all bumped into each other.

Another child said

> One minute we were doing dance and the next minute we were playing this musical statues thing.

Swimming, athletics and outdoor and adventurous activities (OAA) were not seen by the children as being especially linked with the trainees' teaching expertise. This could be due to the involvement of a coach in swimming lessons and the class teacher in athletics and OAA activities.

Interestingly, there was agreement about those trainees whose specialist areas was PE. The children recognized their competence and respected them for it.

> They are proper PE teachers.

> They are more educated about PE

> They work hard because they want to do that particular thing but teachers have to do everything.

It became evident during the course of the interviews that the children perceived trainees who were PE specialists as innovators, providing a range of new experiences but this was less true of non-specialists. This could be related to the scale of this research study or to students preferring to play safe because of control and behavioural concerns. Certainly class teachers who may not have received in-service training in PE for some time look to trainees for new ideas and innovation as a result of their recent experience of training (Lavin 1999; Chapman 1996).

Class control and behaviour

PE teaching presents the trainee teacher with a range of experiences not encountered in the classroom. Children can become very excited; safety issues are to the fore, especially in gymnastics and certain games. Teaching skills required in the hall, playing field and playground are very different from those required in the classroom. Events are unpredictable; teachers must make instant decisions. Trainee teachers are often further handicapped by their lack of knowledge about the pupils' physical abilities.

Pupils clearly perceived a difference between trainees and their class teachers. Some comments focus on the wide range of control that trainees impose.

> Students are nicer, they never tell you off.

> She [the trainee] has to tell some boys off in our class, because they are really naughty.

> She is really strict, you weren't allowed to talk in PE.

Children recognized that some of their peers were difficult to work with. Others felt a real sense of injustice when they perceived they were being treated unfairly:

> If you have a student teacher in you get excited and you talk to your friend and don't listen as much.

The difference between an established classroom teacher and a trainee seeking to establish control is highlighted in this remark:

> All the teachers can take more naughtiness in and then they tell you off, but most student teachers tell you off right away.

The age factor

One factor that was highlighted by the great majority of the children was the age of the trainees and the energy they exhibited in comparison with their class teachers. This seemed to be particularly evident in relation to teaching style, curriculum content and the use of demonstrations. The children appreciated the fact that trainees changed for PE and often were physically involved in the activities. They were, however, understanding about their class teacher's failings in this respect:

> Yeah, they have got more energy, so we can do more things. Yeah you don't see Mrs Granger playing football – no offence to any old teachers!

One of the questions asked of children related to their participation: Is it a good thing that your student teachers join in with you?

> Yeah, gives you more confidence, we all know what to do. If they tell you to do something stupid you don't feel stupid because they are doing it.

The use of demonstrations by the trainees was particularly appreciated by the children:

> Yeah, you just have to copy them really.

The fact that most trainees were younger than their class teacher was seen as a 'good thing' although it was unclear exactly how this factor affected the teaching. One child's comment gave a clue:

> They are younger than the teachers so they remember more games.

Gender

Gender issues were not a concern for the children. The schools in the study all had policies of allowing equal access to the PE curriculum. Some of the girls did complain about not being allowed to do football unless they had football boots. Whether their trainee teacher was a woman or a man was not mentioned as a governing factor in terms of their enjoyment of the subject. However, several studies (Shropshire *et al.* 1997; Chapman 1996) have noted differences in the activities primary children undertake and in self-perception in terms of a 'physical self'. The research provided by the Sports Council (OPCS and Sports Council 1995) showed that differences occur in Years 5 and 6 regarding their perceived ability. Girls were more likely than boys to mind if they perceived themselves as being less able than their peers. More boys than girls wanted to 'win'.

The study by Shropshire *et al.* (1998) on primary-age children found that whilst boys are more willing to participate in physical education, and derive more enjoyment from the subject, girls perceive the physical education teacher as more helpful and kind.

Lessons to be learned from the children

The children interviewed in the study provided a clear view of the way trainee teachers taught PE in primary schools. They enjoyed the new, exciting and fresh ideas. Some of these lessons were quite bizarre. One class of children spoke with awe of the outdoor education lesson in which they had to walk barefoot through deep mud and paint pictures on trees with the same mud. They also enjoyed new dance ideas, sequencing in gymnastics, playing new games and residential experiences.

Children also praised the fairness of trainees. The trainees did not favour the most gifted, but encouraged each child regardless of ability. They were perceived as well meaning in this respect and the children appreciated their fairness. On the less positive side, children often felt that they were being treated unfairly by trainees in terms of allowable behaviour. They did not like trainees who were too strict without a justifiable cause, who did not smile, and who did not praise.

In terms of who the children preferred to be taught by, opinion was divided. Children appreciated the 'with-it-ness' of trainees, and felt some of them were 'cool'. Other preferred the predictability and known qualities of their class teacher.

The message for trainee teachers seems to reflect established good practice:

- Change for PE lessons and join in!
- Respect individual differences and abilities.
- Prepare resources well.

- Prepare appropriate teaching material.
- Develop progression and differentiation.
- Develop a knowledge of the area.
- Encourage positive behaviour and use praise effectively.
- Develop consistent routines.
- Communicate clearly and simply.

The future for PE is under scrutiny in the review of the National Curriculum for the year 2000. It is likely that health-related exercise may be given a higher priority in games, gymnastics and dance. Primary schools are to be given the option of teaching either athletics or outdoor and adventurous activities at Key Stage 2. The children have a view on this. They enjoy all the present components of the NCPE and wish to continue doing them *all*. Perhaps the last word should be left with Rachel (Year 4):

> I like my teacher. She teaches us how to play football and cricket. She's good because she's got a Nike top and trainers.

Suggestions for:

Further investigations

- How important is PE to children in the school curriculum?
  In a circle time at KS1 or a debate at KS2 ask children whether they think PE is important and why. They could design information posters or brochures to explain and share their ideas with other children.

Discussion with mentors in school

- Is PE being marginalized in school because of the focus on the core areas?

Discussion on college-based courses

- The Physical Education Association (PEA UK) have asked for PE to be considered as 'core subject', linked to health and fitness concerns. Is this justified?
- Should the PE curriculum be limited in order to enable teachers to teach fewer areas more effectively?

References

Capel S. (1997) 'Changes in PE students' anxiety on school experience', *European Journal of Physical Education* 2 (2): 198–217.

Chapman V. (1996) 'Ten-year-old children's perceptions of learning with regard to physical activity', *British Journal of Physical Education* 27 (4): 14–17.

Kirk D. (1999) *Girls in Sport*, Loughborough: Youth Sport Trust.

Lavin, J. (1999) 'The implementation of the National Curriculum for Physical Education: Teachers' perceptions and practice', unpublished research.

Ofsted (1998) 'Teaching PE in the Primary School', *The Initial Training of Teachers*, London: HMSO.

Shropshire J., Carroll B. and Yim S. (1997) 'Primary school children's attitudes to Physical Education: Gender differences', *European Journal of Physical Education* 2 (1): 23–38.

Shropshire, J. and Carroll, B. (1998) 'Final year primary school children's physical activity levels and choices', *European Journal of Physical Education* 3(2): 156–66.

Part V
Themes, dimensions and issues

15 'Oh, no – not Jonah again!'

Is aversion to 'Bible story' inevitable?

Lorna Crossman

This chapter is about one small area of religious education (RE), but one that looms so large in the minds of student teachers and children that it tends to colour whole attitudes towards RE. It is the matter of Bible stories.

As a tutor I begin each RE course by asking the students to talk about their own school experience of RE. Although there are always exceptions, RE is frequently and typically regarded as one of the most boring school subjects. My students are no exception. Published studies show that the aversion usually begins from the age of about eight, and that it has one huge focus, 'Ughh – Bible story – and now write about it'. Frequently a compliment paid to the course is 'I'm so glad it wasn't all about Bible story'.

This reflects the content and purposes of RE syllabuses over the years: mainly Christianity and the induction of children into Christianity. Christianity includes the ancient Hebrew stories. Despite the move to an RE curriculum which must now by law include other faiths, Christianity is still expected to absorb at least 50 per cent of the time available. Although content, resources and methodologies have become increasingly diverse, student teachers find that 'Bible story' is still likely to be a large part of that curriculum. The groan, it would seem, is destined to continue.

Yet we cannot just 'drop' story. It is in the nature of all religious traditions that certain key stories are shared by all ages and that they are returned to repeatedly. Much faith community teaching and reflection will be based on an assumed knowledge of these stories, known so well that whole stories can be alluded to with a single name or word or phrase: the Exodus, 'as I brought you out of Egypt', 'Gethsemane', 'the Nativity'; 'Rama'. As Erricker and Green write,

> In one sense religion is story. By this we mean that faith communities are maintained and nourished by the story within which they live.
> (Erricker and Green, 1992: 36)

The one story contains many stories and some of these are so central they are returned to by the faith community in reflection and for reliving in every liturgical year. Indeed, most religious celebrations involve that re-living of a story. The assumption is, therefore, that a community does not tire of its stories, but reinterprets them in every generation. Individuals deepen their understanding throughout a life-time; they grow into the story rather than grow out of it.

In Christian and Hindu communities particularly such stories have been re-presented and lovingly encrusted with artistic jewels – with drama, dance-drama, poetry, painting, sculpture, music. Even in faith communities where the dramatic, musical or visual arts are not associated with sacred texts, those communities have enriched their stories and kept them alive with centuries of liturgy and meditational writing.

A.N. Wilson (1998) writes in his introduction to *The Gospel According to Matthew*:

> Before you apply to it the supposedly rational tests which you would apply to a newspaper report or a television documentary, imagine the chapters which describe the trial and crucifixion of Christ set to music in Bach's St Matthew Passion. Consider the millions of people who over the last 1900 years have recited the prayer [Matthew 6:9–13] which begins 'Our Father'. Think of the old women in Stalin's Russia, when the men were too cowardly to profess their loyalty to the church, who stubbornly continued to chant the opening verses of the Sermon of the Mount in defiance of the KGB. 'Blessed are they that mourn for they shall be comforted' [Matthew 5:4].

It would be difficult for RE teachers to ignore story – nor should they want to. Can we, instead, transform it? Is it pedagogically possible for teachers to learn from faith community practice and enable children to grow into the stories which they re-encounter? Or is it best simply to ensure that, in a school community unsupported by such cultural and spiritual networks, there are few such repetitions? If that is the case, should one withhold many 'Bible stories' from the very young? Or give them to the very young, but make sure they are not repeated with older children?

Bible story in the early years

It would seem easier to use them with the young. For the young do not seem to have an intrinsic aversion to Bible story. Contrary to some student expectations, the young children interviewed for this inquiry were very positive about Bible stories. They said they enjoyed hearing them and enjoyed writing them out. When asked why, it seemed that the Bible story gave a context for mastering skills which mattered to them and about which they were very proud.

I like writing.

At home I read stories and then I write the story.

I like colouring.

I like doing pictures.

In one infant class, composed of Reception and Year 1 children, the student teacher had read several New Testament stories, including Zaccheus, the feeding of the five thousand, the paralysed man whose friends let him down through the roof, and the call of some of the disciples, called 'Jesus' friends'.

The follow-up had been through writing, often consisting of just one sentence with a drawing, ranging from reflection on personal experience to imagining oneself as one of the characters in the story. Children had, for example, following a version of 'the call' of some of 'Jesus' friends' written a piece on 'My best friend is . . .' which ranged from named children, to a teddy bear, to 'Bubble and Squeak' [the pet guinea pigs]. All of these were displayed with pride and pleasure.

Here is Jack's account of 'The Feeding of the Five Thousand':

> One day I went fishing and my mum gave me some bread and then I saw a man on a hill so I climbed the hill and gave Jesus the bread and the fish and the disciples shared them out. And the more they gave out, the more of it was there. I thought amazing. It was like magic.

A fifty-nine word, four-sentence story, but in it Jack has thought himself into being that boy and giving his own imaginary details as to where the fish and the bread came from. The first sentence is sheer succinct time-ordered narrative within the linguistic structures typical of a child of this age. In the second sentence Jack reaches a different dimension and touches the mysterious, and paradoxical, heart of the story:

> and the more they gave out, the more of it was there.

The simplicity of the words convey the wonderment that what should not be possible is possible. That the giving of a little can be greatly multiplied, that the giving of love and friendship does not diminish the supply but increases it, is one of the paradoxical human truths that invert the more normal laws of economic supply and demand. One theological approach to the parables is that they are such inversions and paradoxes. 'Events' in the life of Jesus are seen through theological eyes and in the eyes of Christian communities as parabolic, rather than simply credal. The story and the image become a constant source of moral and spiritual reflection.

Jack ends the story, as he began, in the first person, and then comments

It was like magic.

There are echoes of many New Testament narrative moments here – 'and they were amazed'; 'they marvelled at these things'.

Now we come to Derek Bastide's question: will this story be a *stepping stone* to the children's development of a more mature understanding, or a *stumbling block*? (Bastide 1987:141). Will Jack be helped to get beyond the word 'magic', or will he, as he matures, consider it a story only for little kids – not for those older ones like him who don't believe fairy tales like that any more? Could we be misled – even charmed – by young children's 'enjoyment' and 'ability' into assuming that what can be told should be told? And does the answer depend on the child, or on present and future teachers?

Children in Years 2 and 3 in the same school were still writing 'Bible stories' – and still without any sense of aversion. They had, with their student teacher, Elspeth Bantom, written the story of 'Moses and the Plagues of Egypt' as a straight prose narrative; the story of Samson as a story-board for a video; and the story of Jonah as a comic-strip with speech balloons and 'think bubbles', gloriously and humorously illustrated. Stepping stones or stumbling blocks?

They had enjoyed the variety of the forms of re-telling the stories which Elspeth had introduced. They had enjoyed putting their own collection of stories together as a book and designing covers for them. They had created something they were proud of, books which they were delighted to display. Two children told me that one day they would show them to their own children.

So young children, it seems, do not have an inherent 'problem' with 'Bible stories' or an aversion to them. The stories are still fresh. Re-telling of known stories whatever the source gives young children the opportunity to 'master' the demands of memory, chronology, coherence and literary conventions that story-telling and story-writing demands. The Bible story was seen as another context for 'practising' and 'displaying' these skills. Whether that justifies their use, however, is a more complex matter.

> Simply to tell stories with religious origins may not contribute greatly to a child's religious education however much it stimulates creativity or imparts a moral message. The telling of stories from religious traditions adds to the pupil's store of knowledge, but may not assist religious development.
>
> (Christian Education Movement 1992: 15)

Many would also argue that the problem of literalism – of questioning this story as a possible historical event that one either believes or not –

is not yet a problem for them. As the CEM report comments, 'The distinction, say, between Snow White and the good Samaritan may not be obvious'.

Bible story in the upper-primary years

A group of Year 5 and 6 children articulated their boredom with the stories of Jonah, of 'hearing the same old story all over again'. The transcripts do not begin to convey the intonation and the body language of the children's pronouncements. Interestingly, not one child raised literal belief as a problem. So it might seem obvious that, besides the problem of literalism, sheer repetition is an overwhelming inherent problem. One solution would seem to be, therefore, don't repeat it. This, however, is too simple. For one thing, it leaves the impression that these stories are only fairy tales for the very young; that one needs to grow out of them.

Take the Book of Jonah. It is read in synagogue on the Day of Atonement, the most solemn day of the Jewish year. It cannot be a knock-about narrative about a man apparently swallowed, and spat out again, by a great fish. Insofar as incoherent anger can often be comic to watch or recall, it can be played simply for comedy. But anger and repentance and growth in slow painful understanding also confront us with the depths of human predicaments, anguish and healing, as in King Lear (which has its roots in a fairy tale).

Is it possible to 'play' this story to children at different ages, to help them travel with it from a comic story for three-year-olds, to a sympathetic understanding of why this story is read in its entirety on that most solemn day of the Jewish year? Can we in some sustainable way help our children travel from the 'external events' of the man who was swallowed by a 'great fish', to the inner journey he is making with such pain and such difficulty? Can we lead young people towards the solemn psalmic beauty of his prayer from the depths in Chapter 2, and hear in it the tragedies and recoveries of personal and community stories? Can we help our children travel towards the extraordinary dialogues of Chapter 4:

> I know that you are a gracious God and merciful, slow to anger and abounding in steadfast love, and ready to relent from punishing. And now, please take my life from me, for it is better for me to die than live.
> And the Lord said, 'Is it right for you to be angry?'

Such stories and their 'eternal return' are at the heart of RE. In the secular world we give the fairy-tale to young children but we keep King Lear for the far more mature. Can we sustain a religious story into maturity?

My interviews with upper-primary children and their accounts of student teachers, hint that the problem of repetition is not inherent in the story, but within the pedagogy, especially at the key points of delivery and follow-up.

Delivery of Bible story

All these older primary children talked about how long the readings were.

Sometimes teachers read on and on and on.

This statement was made in virtually identical words by upper primary children who had wowed a church congregation with their version of the Creation; children who had loved dramatic renderings of the story of Moses; and by the children who expressed sheer boredom with Jonah. They described getting tired and fidgety, and being unable to listen any longer. It is difficult to give quotations here for children mimicked such readings through their intonations and gestures. They were funny, and rather scurrilous, and got the point across marvellously!

Two groups of children interviewed contrasted the very positive experiences of story they had had with their student teachers, with what 'normally happened'. The student teachers, Jane Henderson and Heather Grey, treated story-telling and story-reading as one of the expressive arts.

One Year 6 class had worked on the story of Moses, particularly his confrontation with the Pharaoh, which they already knew. It did not matter. The accolades flew:

> She reads it so it goes in your mind and stays with you.
> She changes voice to suit the person and the episode.
> She makes you hear it too.
> She emphasizes a lot more with her voice.
> She was so expressive.
> She enjoys herself and you enjoy it too.
> Normally we just read stuff out of the Bible, on and on and on, and it gets on my nerves.

Meanwhile, in a tiny, two-class, Church of England village school on the edge of rolling moors, student teacher Sally Jackson came near to doing the local vicar out of his Sunday job. There was so much laughter and excitement in telling about this event that it was difficult to piece it all together. The vicar, unable to be present on a particular Sunday morning, and with no substitute available, had appealed to the children to lay something on. Determined not to think small, Sally and the children rendered the Creation story into 'modern words' and each of the children took parts. They had greatly appreciated her dramatic approach, how she showed them how to be more and more expressive with their bodies and voices. They loved the success and the response:

They were all laughing.
They said it was the most interesting thing they had ever had.
It was great.

The performance of the Creation had erupted, unplanned, into the block practice.

Sally Jackson's general attitude and her planned RE work involved the same appreciated features. The children spoke of her and of her teaching with enthusiasm and delight. They had particularly enjoyed the drama and dance and the way she had run a tap-dancing class after school hours.

And even the boys wanted to join in!
She 'made everything fun and interesting'.

Sally brought this obvious flair for drama and dance to everything she did – and that included her RE which was not excluded from this lively, engaged teaching in the name of 'piety' or 'fear of getting it wrong'.

Following the story

'Writing it' was the most frequently cited follow-up for upper-primary children – and they hated it. They had got beyond the stage where practising writing for its own sake, for mastery and competence, was satisfying. What had given the infants delight no longer brought any pleasure. The delight in a story heard only once or twice before has gone. Writing simply to show that you can is not sufficient at this age, no longer a satisfaction in itself; it has lost its 'cognitive challenge'. It is as though these children are describing an endless diet of bread that has long gone stale.

The dread of the length and monotony of readings was mirrored by the dread and dislike of the writing:

Your hand just aches.
You just get sick of doing it.
Normally it's just 'write, write, write'.

And indeed, this becomes more understandable if one remembers their dislike of a reading which goes 'on and on and on', never broken into episodes for discussion or reflection. The writing out of an epic-length story (especially if it has already bored you to death) becomes a dreaded and sterile task.

Nothing changes – you write down for the umpteenth time what you already know; what the teacher already knows; what you know she knows you know. They rarely experienced variety; nor do the writing tasks seem to have purpose or progress. The children who described Jonah in such 'turned off' terms had never been asked to write a poem to freeze-frame one moment of it, or one mood from it. They had never been asked to think of how they would present it as a drama. They had never heard a poem or song based on it; had never experienced a reflection on Jonah by a Jewish scholar; had never related it to moments and challenges in their own life. They could no longer even think of alternatives to 'writing it', but their body language changed as I [rather exceeding my brief!], suggested some of these possibilities and asked if it would change the story for them.

Teachers who require this usual sort of writing during RE have not drawn on the insights of the English curriculum:

- that writing must have a purpose and can be done in a vast variety of forms;
- that, in particular, writing can be reflective and responsive in its focus rather than simply narrative;
- that it must have criteria for success and progress beyond that of length or spelling, etc;
- that writing need not be a silent and solitary activity;
- and that stories can be explored through means other than writing.

The children who were studying Moses with Jane Henderson said:

> We acted out Moses – we were allowed to dress up – she made us be really expressive.
> Normally it's just 'write, write, write'.

They had enjoyed these opportunities for drama, and that Jane had modelled and encouraged the expressiveness she had shown in her own original renderings.

They had also produced it as an assembly and again the comparisons flew:

> Her assemblies were brilliant.
> Normally we just do silly, boring things and the infants just sit there bored and going to sleep.
> But we all had action parts and had to be expressive and we acted it out instead of just doing it straight like and we changed the version to make it funny and modern.

In historical terms we could say that Jane Henderson, like Sally Jackson who worked with the Creation story, had acted in the tradition of the medieval mystery plays, making the story 'modern', living and vivid, and not being afraid to include humour.

Jane had also set the story in a specifically Jewish context and introduced the children to the Passover. They had seen and then made models of a Seder plate, using paper 'flaps' for the hollows and revealing the symbolic foods beneath the flaps. These had been beautifully decorated and the children showed them to me with pride. They had made mobiles that were constructed of their own illustrated food metaphors for friends using very modern imagery – 'You're greater than a Big Mac'. Moses had been set in its Jewish context; had led to knowledge about the Passover; had been enriched with artefacts; had used their own experience of friendship to deepen an understanding of metaphoric language, particularly that centring on food. They had enjoyed the construction of things and the imaginative brevity of the writing form which then became 3-D art works. While making the constructions they had listened to music and said they found that very peaceful and helped their concentration.

One child in this group asked,

> Why can't all teachers be more imaginative in the things they ask us to do? Why is it always just 'write, write, write'?

and others added,

> This will stay in our memory … we will remember this even when we go to secondary school.
> She's got such a good imagination.
> She brings new ideas into our heads.

These children were very far from 'negotiating down'; every word they uttered conveyed the sense of fun, a sense of much needed cognitive challenge being met.

These highly dramatic approaches are not the only way. Simply giving the children the chance to ask the questions and to try out their answers instead of the teacher asking the questions can transform the boring into the interesting.

Of a lesson in a Year 2 class of a Church of England school, Michael Shepherd, a student teacher, reports:

> When the lesson finished some of the children didn't want to go out to play, but to continue with RE which I thought was a special moment for me.

What had they been doing? Thinking of questions they'd like to ask God!

* How did you think of making this world?
* How did you make yourself?
* Are angels your helpers?
* How do you get everywhere?

- Why did you choose Mary to have Jesus?
- How can you listen to everybody at the same time?
- How old are you?
- How did you get your magic powers?

And many more.

These were not questions for the student teacher to answer, nor for him to evaluate, or for him to 'correct' the answers offered; they were real questions for real discussion. Theologians have struggled with some of them.

Michael Shepherd writes:

> Both myself and the children enjoyed this activity as it is something they had not done before. ... The children were coming up to me throughout the day, telling me they had thought of lots of questions and I was pleased the children had something to take away and think about.

An infant class in an urban school had been first introduced to the Torah as an artefact. My interview with this group of children was actually some weeks after the event, but, with their colour drawings to trigger their memories, they still talked with enthusiasm of the experience of seeing a Torah scroll in its beautiful covering.

> We opened it and saw all the little writing.
> Yeah – and we drawed the scroll and the cupboard.
> And we maked one.

They remembered also their discussion of the commandments. Here they are as translated and remembered by Key Stage 1 children:

> No stealing
> No fighting
> Don't mess
> Be good to your parents
> Don't swear
> Don't run away
> Don't rob
> and
> Don't nick!

There were no visual memory triggers for this rendition. The children reconstructed it together. There were no worksheets, no meaningless recitations of commandments they could not possibly understand.

Conclusions

By using the arts curriculum, particularly art and drama, and by thinking of writing tasks that did not depend on children having to 'write, write, write' with no sense of purpose, by contextualizing stories, using artefacts connected with the re-telling and re-living of those stories, student teachers engaged children of every age in their RE work. Aversion to RE can be prevented and reversed.

Among upper-primary children, the huge negativity towards Bible story can be prevented by more imaginative approaches: reading and telling as expressive arts, as 'the giving of a gift' (King 1992: 155) and journeying within these stories by means of the whole arts curriculum. The longer the time allocated to the exploration of one story, the more chance there is that response can be reflective. This does not mean, however, that the response has to be a lengthy product. A three-line, seventeen-syllable Haiku may represent more thought and reflection than a three-page 'recitation' of sequenced events.

Faith stories are stories of living communities; they have inspired some of the great drama, art, poetry, painting, music of the world. They have inspired radical political movements. Martin Luther King, for example, constantly alluded to the Exodus story. Every student teacher can bring life to the telling and rich imagination to the 'follow-up'. Even where constraints of school syllabus, time-table and expectations seem to demand what student teachers least want to do, children and students can be turned around by fresh and innovative practice in story itself. Bible story transformed becomes transforming.

Suggestions for:

Further reading

Francis, L. (1979) 'The child's attitude towards religion: A review of research', *Educational Research* 21(2): 103–108.

Minney, R. (1985) 'Why are pupils bored in RE?', *British Journal of Educational Studies* 33(3): 250–261.

On the use of story in RE

Bastide, D. (1987) *Religious Education 5–12*, London: Falmer Press. (See especially chapters 11–14.)

Cole, W.O. and Evans-Lowndes, J. (1991) *Religious Education in the Primary Curriculum*, Exeter: RMEP. (See especially chapter 10.)

Copley, T. (1994) *Religious Education 7–11: Developing Primary Teaching Skills*, London, Routledge. (See especially Unit 3.)

Further investigations

- Take one 'Biblical' story for example a parable [or 'Jonah'!] and find editions of it ranging from a target audience of pre-school children to a target audience of adults. Do the books 'progress' other than linguistically? If yes – what does this reveal about progressive under-standing? If no – what are the implications?
- Read the story of Jonah written in the Bible. Give an account of it to someone else without naming the external narrative events – 'It's about a man who . . .'?

Discussion with mentors in school

Thinking about story

- If the whole story is an epic – for example the story of Moses or the Ramayana – how thoughtfully and effectively are you working at breaking it into manageable, interesting episodes that give children the chance for reflecting on and feeling each development and theme?
- How well are you selecting your story (or episode) for its purpose, and its potential for reflections with the children?
- To what extent do you not just 'allow' but encourage the children to ask the questions and voice their responses afterwards and to what extent do you enable them to discuss one another's questions and responses rather then you acting as a 'tester', or the authoritative imposer of interpretations?

Discussion on college-based courses

- How far does the material in this chapter reflect your own experience of (a) being a pupil yourself? (b) being a student teacher in a school?
- Jerome Bruner wrote: 'We might ask, as a criterion for any subject taught in primary school, whether, when fully developed, it is worth an adult's knowing, and whether having known it as a child makes a person a better adult. If the answer to both questions is negative or ambiguous, then the material is cluttering the curriculum'. (Bruner 1963: 52). How does RE fare under this criterion?
- Have you grown in understanding of any story you know well? (not necessarily a religious story).

References

Bastide, D. (1987) *Religious Education 5–12*, London: Falmer.
Bruner, J. (1963) *The Process of Education*, New York: Vintage.
Christian Education Movement (1992) *Implementing Religious Education Five to Sixteen*, Derby: Christian Education Movement.

Erricker C. and Green, R. (1992) 'A journey with Ganesh', *Multi-Cultural Teaching* 10(2): 36–38.

King, C. (1992) 'The place of Story in RE', in D. Bastide (ed.) *Good Practice in Primary Religious Education*, London: Falmer Press.

Wilson, A. N. (1998) Introduction in *The Gospel According to Matthew*, Edinburgh: Canongate.

16 'Solicitous tenderness'*

Discipline and responsibility in the classroom

Kate Jacques

How do children assess a student's ability to control and manage the whole class and how do they respond? How does the student assess the mood, the tone of the class and then decide how to manage behaviour?

It is no surprise that student teachers repeatedly highlight discipline and problem behaviour as their most serious concerns. When asked to talk about 'poor teachers', children and teachers most often identify inability to keep control as the most serious shortcoming. When mentors assess students they frequently point to discipline problems as the major weakness and lack of control as a performance indicator over most other reasons. Headteachers perceive high noise levels as a clear signal that things are not going well. When talking to potential candidates for teacher training, one of their major concerns is the issue of discipline and the much publicized deterioration in pupil behaviour. This preoccupation with discipline has come under even sharper focus recently as sixth formers and graduates explain to careers tutors that they are reluctant to go into teaching because they are worried about controlling the class and facing verbal abuse meted out by difficult pupils. They refer to television and media coverage about life in schools. They have confusing and mixed pictures of violence and disruption in schools, and of high achievement and hard work. But it is the negative images that seem to remain longest. While many young people are content with their own school, they believe that behaviour is worse in other schools and that, in general, schools these days are tough places to be. The fact that the overwhelming majority of primary and secondary schools are communities of well-managed, well-organized groups of people engaged in learning and teaching with a focus on achievement, is not the prevailing image. But young people who rise above the negative media images and accept the challenge must nevertheless manage children while educating them and develop their own individual successful teaching style. In this chapter I explore the question of discipline and behaviour and what children have to say. It is the part

* Pye, D. (1988: 92)

of the job of teaching which is most misunderstood by students and perhaps the least well taught on training courses. Children are very clear about what they expect from a good teacher, and contrary to popular belief, they like and want an orderly classroom.

It is worth pausing to determine what we mean by some of the terms used in this context. 'Discipline' and 'control' are frequently used interchangeably but this is wrong: they mean different things. Discipline implies good order and complicity about agreed behaviour. Control implies power and containment, and depends centrally on teacher authority. Behaviour management similarly suggests that the teacher has power over the pupils who have to be handled in a certain way to ensure compliance. The teacher, of course, is in a position of power and is able to control events but the children can wield a subversive power. Disruption in various forms is their strategy. I shall use the terms 'discipline' and 'responsibility' to describe both pupil and student teachers' classroom skills. If classroom order depends entirely on control, there will be problems. Bewildering messages surround the whole area and students are told conflicting things by different people. For example, it is likely in college that students will be told if they know their subject they will have few discipline problems, that subject knowledge and sound preparation are the keys. A contrary message will contain advice about 'Don't try to teach a subject until you can control the class'. Another common guide is 'With a new class, don't smile until after Christmas'. Additional tips include 'Be firm', 'Don't be too friendly', 'Let them know who is boss', 'Be sympathetic'. There is always a long list. These tips may be useful but that is all they are – tips. They are no substitute for thoughtful, carefully worked out strategies. The complexity of teaching is part of the misunderstanding about maintaining discipline. Sound discipline is largely about being an effective and efficient teacher and being an effective and efficient teacher is more about what the pupils think of the teacher than the other way round. As we shall see later, pupils detect very quickly what the teacher thinks of them individually and as a class and they relate this to teacher competence. That competence is not only about preparation, planning and subject knowledge, it is about teachers knowing who they are, being confident in their relationships with pupils and in their own interpersonal skills. Newly qualified teachers believe that their training did not include sufficient preparation on how to control a class. They seem to believe that there is a fool-proof recipe which their tutors refuse to tell them. Conceptualizing classroom order in terms of 'control' is central to the problem.

The fact that discipline and control are so often used interchangeably when in fact they are conceptually different is important for student teachers to understand. Students tend to believe that success has been achieved once they are in control and remain in control. Logically this implies that a battle has been fought and won – the student teachers have

by one means or another established power over the class and all individuals therein. The problem with this strategy is that it requires constant
vigilance and law enforcement tactics such as systems of reward and
punishment. It is essentially punitive – teacher and taught see themselves
as lining up on different sides. Such a regime takes an enormous amount
of energy to maintain and relates only indirectly to the educational activity
of the classroom. Controlling behaviour becomes exhausting and does not
promote a good classroom climate. A disciplined classroom on the other
hand is one in which everyone shares the same goals and intentions. In
a disciplined environment there are broadly agreed assumptions between
teacher and pupils about the common purposes of the classroom.
Variations will exist but the general tenor of the classroom is one in which
everyone understands why they're there. That is not to say that there will
not be violations from time to time. But good behaviour is expected from
everyone including the teacher. There is, however, a powerfully held view
communicated often passionately by politicians and the media that classrooms must be controlled. Failing schools are characterized by children
'out of control'. There is pressure on teachers to move away from a child-
centred, liberal-democratic regime to a more authoritarian, competitive,
achievement-orientated climate. Standard Attainment Test results, leagues
tables and parental pressure have fundamentally changed what was once
perceived to be a gentle, *laissez-faire* attitude to teaching and learning in
primary schools. Anne Yoe, the chair of the Parent Teacher Associations,
said that she was convinced primary teachers wanted to make children
happy but there was little evidence that they wanted children to learn
very much (Yoe 1991). To this point and others we shall return, but for
now let's look at what the pupils talked about during the inquiry.

I was interested in what children think about how student teachers
manage pupil behaviour. There are studies which look at pupil attitudes
to classroom teachers (for example Wragg, 1993) but few which look at
pupil attitudes to student teachers.

What pupils said about student teachers and discipline

To explore what children think about discipline and student teachers,
three groups of ten to twelve children from three different schools spent
an hour and a half in discussion prompted by five open-ended questions.
They were all Year 6 children, chosen by the class teacher as likely to
talk readily with an interviewer. They were not necessarily the brightest,
but children most likely, in the teacher's view, to have an opinion and
be willing to express it.

The three schools in the sample were approached because they were
highly supportive of school-based training and the partnership between
the college and school, and because they represented three different types
of school. Moss Crag school is a small, rural, three-teacher school located

in a village. Prestwick Road is an urban, multicultural school of 388 pupils and Manor Park is a large, suburban school of 502 pupils named as a Beacon School.

The group interviews took place either in the headteacher's study or in an empty classroom. The children were withdrawn from a class it was felt that they could miss without problems.

Once assembled, I explained that they had been chosen to talk about what they felt about student teachers and classroom discipline and that I would ask some questions to help get a conversation going. The questions were:

1   Do you know how people learn to become teachers?
2   Do you know what people learn when they train to become teachers?
3   Do you know when you are being taught by a student teacher? If so, how?
4   What are the best things about being taught by a student teacher?
5   What is not so good about student teachers?

The answers and the pattern of the discussions had similar threads (these will be addressed later) but there were also some interesting differences, which might go some way to substantiating what students often say about the importance of the school in which they are placed on school experience and judgements about their work vary according to the people in the school.

Crag Moss

The children were a curious mix of those who wanted to give serious answers and those who wanted to tell me about the difficult time they deliberately gave student teachers. Because it was a small school serving a village community of families from a variety of backgrounds, different attitudes emerged.

Most of the children said they thought students went to university to learn about teaching and then had to practise in school with children 'to learn how to punish them!'. Further probing revealed that new teachers had to learn a lot but it was mainly about how to stop children 'mucking about'. The children used the word 'punish' a great deal.

The group confirmed that they all knew when they had a student teacher because their proper teacher did not always trust them and 'hung about cleaning cupboards' and 'cutting up paper'. If there was noise she turned around and 'looked'!

They were able to distinguish clearly between a supply teacher and a student teacher. They had a regular, well-known supply teacher who was 'the same as the staff'. Students were spotted immediately and testing started from day one! The testing, however, was guided entirely by the behaviour of the students.

Pupils self evidently welcome a lively teacher who can introduce new and exciting areas of interest or new ways of learning about standard curriculum matters.

What they described however, in answer to 'what's not so good about student teachers?' was disappointment with a student teacher who 'could not control the class or tried to be too friendly'. Further discussion suggested that they thought it was very important that the student had authority over the class. Two children referred to an example where they felt the class teacher did not have much confidence in the student teacher and so the class did not either. Again, the group referred to the need for the class teacher to be around in the class if the student teacher 'was being too easy'.

The ten children in this group spoke affectionately about their student teachers especially the two that were in the school at the time of the interview. Nevertheless they were clear that they did not like students that put them down or showed them up. 'If a teacher is not fair I do not like that, especially if I get blamed for something I did not do'.

Prestwick Road

The children made many similar points but there were some differences. As a large city-centre primary school with a large Asian Muslim population, some expectations of the children were different but nevertheless focused heavily on discipline and control.

The children were less certain about how teachers were trained. They said they thought that teachers went to college but were not sure. This school takes a large number of student teachers throughout the year and the children seemed to take for granted that they were just there. The children said they liked having more teachers in the classroom because 'you get more attention in groups'. In answer to the question about what do student teachers learn to do, the response again was largely about the perceived need to control the class. 'Teachers have to learn how to control the children or they cannot teach anything', 'it is important that children obey the teacher at all times. If the teacher is not obeyed the class does not learn.'

The group agreed that obeying the teacher was important and when asked if they knew when they were being taught by a student they said gleefully that they had loads of student teachers and that some of them did not know how to be obeyed.

The children liked being taught in small groups by student teachers because they got a lot more attention and they all felt they needed more help. They also mentioned that some student teachers were really good at new work and that they did some great things which their class teacher did not do.

In answer to the final question about what was not so good, they too did not like student teachers who 'put them down' or 'shout at children in front of the whole class'. Along with the previous group, they thought the teacher should be strict but fair. They said that they did not mind teachers who were strict but they disliked teachers who had favourites and were unfair in other ways.

Manor Park

Manor Park, by contrast, is not in a wealthy, leafy suburb but it is located in a relatively stable, out-of-town private and council housing estate. The school has done exceptionally well in Ofsted inspections and been identified as a Beacon School.

The twelve children in this group were different from the others in that they offered many more comments without first being asked. This school receives significant numbers of student teachers, sometimes as many as eight at a time. The children encounter a greater variety and observe differences in students keenly. Before talking to the children the deputy head was emphatic that children did not know the difference between student teachers and supply teachers. The staff were at pains to welcome students as if they were teachers. This was deliberate so as not to affect the status of students in the eyes of the children. In answer to the question about how teachers are trained, it was fascinating to hear them say that they knew teachers went to college but they also 'learn in our school'. 'We get loads of students' said one child. 'There is one in our class now. I like him but he is not as good as Mr Weaver [the class teacher].' The group were very clear about why the class teacher had the edge. Children made statements such as 'He's nice but he can't really control us all the time'; 'When we muck about he shouts and loses his temper'. 'He isn't funny like Mr Weaver'; 'He tells us off even when it's not our fault'.

When asked how did they know the difference between a student teacher and a real teacher one boy said 'We just do, you can tell'. Various descriptions were offered, many of which contradicted each other. 'They are nervous', 'Do new work', 'They do too easy work', 'They shout a lot', 'Aren't strict enough', 'Too bossy', 'Not fair', 'Have favourites'. It became clear that, whether effective or not, the children were able to recognize student teachers, that there were characteristics they liked and others which they did not.

In response to the question about what students had to learn to become teachers, they, like the previous groups, concentrated almost entirely on discipline. 'They have to control the class and punish bad children' one girl said. Another said 'Students have to make children do as they are told'. 'They have to make us work'. This preoccupation with discipline and control was at the same time interspersed with 'We like kindness', 'We like fun', 'We like students who are fair' – all suggesting that the way they are treated as a class and as individuals matters a great deal and affects their approach to what they do in lessons.

Analysis of the interviews

From the three very lively conversations about student teachers some fascinating pupil perceptions emerged. Three, however, stand out as worthy of further scrutiny.

1   Children can suss out a student teacher before they push open the school gate. No matter how confident, or prepared, or what labels are used or not used, they know. What happens depends on how the student deals with things.
2   Pupils see the ability to manage class behaviour as key to student survival and from what they say that relationship is critical.
3   Students have the potential to affect pupil learning much more than they realize. Pupils want to be challenged – when they are, then they are less inclined 'to muck about'.

Most of the children enjoyed having students in their classrooms because, according to them, they planned and prepared new and different sorts of lessons. It was the students who did not do new or imaginative things who attracted most criticism. When lessons did not keep the children busy, they had two strategies: mucking about to ward off boredom, or pretending to make the work last so that no other work would be provided. Children worked out very quickly when insufficient work had been prepared and they knew how to exploit the opportunities offered.

Children know when students do not have sufficient subject knowledge; in some cases the children believed that they knew more than the student. In one school the children cited an example where a student got some mathematics wrong because according to the main speaker, 'She didn't know her tables'. He went on to say 'We did, and we used to give her the wrong answers but she didn't know they were wrong. She would get confused and then we would start mucking about and laughing.' (The student teacher in question did have to withdraw from the course but this illustrates that pupils are not easily fooled.)

Students who were warm and accepting, enthusiastic and inspiring, were the most popular. Children mentioned students who took time to talk to them as individuals, who listened, who respected their ideas and suggestions. A sense of humour was frequently mentioned as a reason for working hard for a teacher. Being fair was important. Children did not like student teachers who were cold and distant, bad tempered and always shouting, who never smiled, who never engaged in casual conversations.

Temperament emerged as something children could exploit for their own ends. Clearly some student teachers will have a shorter fuse than others. Some children, it seems, find it amusing if they can make the students lose their temper. All sorts of reasons create conditions where losing one's temper may be an option, but children find it unacceptable when teachers lose their temper and their reaction is largely to laugh. However, the most frequently criticized strategy was 'putting you down'. Students who humiliate children in front of the whole class were the ones disliked most. This was agreed by the children in all three schools. Various examples of humiliation were cited: being made to stand up in front of the whole class, being insulted, work being criticized. Over-bossiness was disliked and they recognized that students who could not keep control tried to be bossy and to pretend to be in charge when they were not.

While 'confidence' was not a word the children used, the meaning came through in the way they described 'the "something" that real teachers have and that students don't'. Pushed to describe this 'something' they talked about some teachers having eyes in the back of their head, knowing what was going to happen before it happened, appearing to understand the way children behaved, and rarely being surprised or upset. Taking things in one's stride probably comes closest to describing this inner confidence. This quality appears to be something that is acquired over time and perhaps is the single, most prevalent factor which tells a class of children the difference between a student and an experienced teacher.

Children did comment on the different strategies used by male and female students to maintain order and discipline. The extent to which gender stereotyping of teachers enters pupils' consciousness is an important question and one which may not be recognized. It emerged that in general, although not always specifically, they thought male students were more relaxed, likely to have a greater sense of humour and always fair. Several children mentioned that female students were not as fair as male students. Examples of this lack of fairness were: punishing the whole class (everyone loses their playtime) for something only two or three people had done; telling off large groups of people when only one person was guilty; not listening to the full story before making a judgement. It would be difficult to judge the accuracy of these perceptions when experience would indicate that events such as those described are distributed across the classrooms of both male and female students.

So what conclusions can be drawn?

The significance of my analysis is the extent to which student teachers are able to ensure effective pupil learning while learning themselves how to manage pupil behaviour and attitudes to learning. Knowing how to use one's own style and personality to best effect in creating a positive classroom climate takes time. Learning to raise levels of subject knowledge is easier to manage, but in a sense all the issues which children raised were not new or surprising. Most students themselves can remember the characteristics they liked and did not like in their own teachers. So, can all students learn to promote good classroom discipline? The answer is yes, so long as students recognize their need for self-discipline. For example, respect cannot be learned if the children are not treated with respect. Students need to ask themselves 'How do I come across to this class of children? Do the class regard me as respecting their ideas, each one as an individual? Am I always scrupulously fair?' We know that an ill-tempered attitude generates hostility and a reluctance to work. A positive and supportive climate gets results. To create a good positive working environment in which all children are motivated and involved in carrying out the planned work and not creating disruption is dependent to a large extent on the ethos and the mutuality of regard in which teacher and taught hold each other.

When in difficulties student teachers will frequently believe that the problem lies with the children, but the children see the problem as being with the student. Conversations with children reveal how students frequently underestimate the powerful impact they have on children. 'As a teacher I possess tremendous power to make a child's life miserable or joyous. I can be a tool of torture or an instrument of inspiration. I can humiliate, humour, hurt or heal' (Ginott 1992). Morgan and Morris (1999), in their study of pupils' and teachers' views of each other, identify that teachers need to recognize their powerful effect on children's ability to learn and on how children view themselves.

Certain children have a tougher time in achieving. They require more energy and attention and that precious extra time and attention are the important ingredients. There is a tendency among some teachers to believe that certain children whom they label 'disadvantaged' will not learn, will be unmotivated and that nothing the school can do will affect this position. Morgan and Morris (1999) found that teachers were unaware of the effect they had on difficult children, believing that the individuals and the class determined the success of lessons. The children were very clear that some teachers were more effective and successful than others simply because of the way they treated their pupils. This is an important lesson for all students. Children can be unaware that it is their own personal approach which affects their learning They perceive it to be the job of the teachers, while teachers see pupil ability as being the most significant factor. In order for children to believe in themselves they need to believe in the teachers. The children Morgan and Morris talked to identified good order and discipline as the key factors in creating a positive classroom ethos. They also mentioned the things that the children I interviewed mentioned: good humour, fairness, trust, good relationships, respect. Pye (1998: 92) calls this 'solicitous tenderness' and argues that this is the foundation of good relationships in classrooms. This tenderness, he claims, helps children to believe in themselves.

This notion of mutual respect has been a fundamental precept of education since 1798 when Kant argued that respect for persons was the basis for sound law and order (Abbott 1940). The theme was generated in the middle of the twentieth century by the educational philosopher R. S. Peters, who suggested that disorderly classrooms need not exist if the ethos was guided by the notion of respect and human regard. Clearly life is more complicated than this and at the beginning of the twenty-first century is likely to become more so. As we described at the beginning, so many variables enter the lives of both children and student teachers that having a high regard for everybody all the time will not eradicate some of the serious social problems with which people have to deal. It is argued here, however, that such a philosophy will go a significant way towards helping a student manage successfully the primary classroom. The various pieces of advice given to students about keeping control disappear into irrelevance if it is recognized that attitude and understanding are far more important at the outset than actual conduct.

Suggestions for:

Further reading

Blandford, S. (1998) *Managing Discipline in Schools*, London: Routledge. Good on theory and practical application. Heavy in parts and not an easy read but quite inspirational.

Barnerd, S. (1998) *Developing Children's Behaviour in the Classroom, A Practical Guide for Teachers and Students*, London: Falmer Press. Some of you will love this book. It says some profound things about Special Educational Needs and strategies amongst teachers for dealing with such difficulties. Others amongst you will wonder about the need for a systematic approach to learning because it is unconventional.

McGuinness, J. (1993) *Teachers, Pupils and Behaviour. A Managerial Approach*, London: Cassell. My favourite. This is not a tips for teachers course but the book conveys a deep understanding about people especially children and teachers. He renews one's belief that in the end children's self-esteem matters more than SATs results and league tables.

Morgan, C. and Morris, G., (1999) *Good Teaching and Learning: Pupils and Teachers Speak*, Buckingham: Open University Press. For students, the results of this research are first rate. It gets to the heart of what pupils and teachers think about teachers. However, it is better read the year following the first year and it has a Secondary perspective.

Rogers, B. (1998) *You Know the Fair Rule*, London: Pitman Publishing. Lots of good advice on strategies to make behaviour management easier and in some cases good fun.

Hopkins, D., West, M., and Ainscow, N. *et al.*, (1997) *Creating the Conditions for Classroom Improvement*, London: David Fulton. A book of INSET ideas beyond behaviour and discipline. Some good ideas for improving relationships and classroom climates.

Further investigations

One way to find out why pupils behave badly in classrooms is to ask them. Construct a brief questionnaire which asks children about poor behaviour and why it happens. The questions need to be simple and straightforward and easy to answer. For example:

- When were you last punished in class for misbehaviour?
- What did you do wrong?
- Why did you do it?
- Was the punishment fair?

Arrange small group discussions about what pupils think make good teachers.

Discussion with mentors in school

- Personality matters! How do I use my own personal style to best effect in managing the class?
- How do I learn to get 'eyes in the back of my head'?
- How do I learn to ignore trivial minor disruption while dealing effectively with critical serious incidents?
- Which qualities need developing to gain the interest and attention of the class?
- Are there any characteristics which I have in teaching which are negative and which I need to tackle?

Discussion on college-based courses

- In what ways is behaviour management different from behaviour control?
- Brainstorm ways in which you can promote respect and trust in the classroom regardless of race, colour, creed, age, disability, ability or appearance.
- Share your investigation findings under the headings: qualities children rate highly in a good teacher; qualities which they rate poorly. Are there common factors?

References

Abbott, T. K. (1940) *Fundamental Principles of Metaphysics Of Morals*, London: Longman.

Ginott, H. (1992), in B. Rogers (1998) *You Know the Fair Rule*, London: Pitman Publishing, p. 7

Morgan, C. and Morris, G. (1999) *Good Teaching and Learning: Pupils and Teachers Speak*, Buckingham: Open University Press.

Pye, J. (1998) *Invisible Children*, Oxford: Oxford University Press.

Wragg, E. C. (1994) 'Pupils' view of management', in J. Bourne, *Thinking Through Primary Practice*, London: Routledge/Open University.

—— (1984) *Classroom Teaching Skills*, London: Croom Helm.

Yoe, E. (1991) 'The rise and fall of primary education' in A. Pollard and J. Bourne (eds) (1994) *Teaching and Learning in the Primary School*, London: Routledge.

17 Please Sir! Yes Miss!

Owain Evans

Nicknames 'Sir' and 'Miss' fulfil the formal requirements of schools where first names for teachers are never used by either children or adults. And the respectful sub-text of Sir eclipses the soubriquet Miss. Time was, and recently, when that sub-text translated into reality. Men who trained to be primary-school teachers did so with the sure expectation of a head-ship. Now, as we all know, the playing field has been levelled. For instance, of Hackney's fifty-eight primary schools, forty-three have women heads.

The teaching staff of secondary schools more closely reflect the male/female profile of our population. This has never been true in primary schools. At St Martin's 85 per cent of the primary trainees are women, this proportion has remained fairly static over the last decade and is probably representative of Initial Teacher Training institutions as a whole. A nation-wide campaign in 1998 by the Teacher Training Agency and the National Union of Teachers revealed that whereas 40 per cent of 'A' Level girls would consider becoming teachers, only 9 per cent of the boys identified it as a possible career option. Men training for primary-school teaching face a double dilemma. They may do one or more of their placements in schools where the staff are all women, some of whom may construct men teachers in a negative way. A headteacher: 'ineffective and ineffectual'. A parent: 'not a fit job for a man'. In other school placements a man, simply by virtue of being male, may be burdened with expectations of authority and wisdom, expectations that are unfair to him and to his fellow trainees who are women. There is also an undercurrent of suspicion attached to men in the teaching profession, as a second-year student noted on a recent teaching practice:

> When I first met the Head he said that I must never be alone with a child, and that if a child was unwell or injured on no account was I to touch them or comfort them. He never said that to the female trainees, so I must be considered a potential monster.

Experiences such as this must introduce an unwarranted state of anxiety in our young male trainees that does not assist the development of a healthy rapport between themselves and their pupils. Problematic too is the influence of the long-running campaign entitled 'Stranger danger' with its emphasis upon unknown men having evil intent, especially when the evidence indicates that a high proportion of the attacks upon children are carried out by people well known to the child so abused. Certainly it must be of concern to everyone that there has been a rise in the number of men convicted for abusing their position of care and trust within the school system, although far more commonly that happens elsewhere.

- As a trainee what advice and guidance have you received regarding your relationship with children in your care? How comfortable do you feel accepting the requirement to be 'in loco parentis'?
- Have you ever felt that your role with a child has moved from being the teacher to being a surrogate parent?

How are we to know what influence being a man or a woman has on our pupils? Each relationship in the classroom is unique and has a multiplicity of complexions and that characteristic which encourages a constructive rapport in one case may not in others. There are combinations of personal characteristics, prior experiences and contextual influences that make any examination of a given behaviour or an expressed opinion very tenuous. However simply to accept that this conundrum exists would not have been helpful. I still believed that it was worth making some attempt to assess the children's perceptions of working with a male trainee. So I arranged to interview pupils that had recently been taught by male trainees. The schools were chosen to represent a wide variety of placement including small schools with two teachers and large ones with three-form entry. Some were very rural and others were in the cities. Some had all female staff, some were mixed, some had female headteachers. The fifty-two children interviewed were from Year 2 to Year 6. I noted those who had any previous experience of working with male teachers. The trainees who taught them included some from each year of our four-year degree course and also members of the post-graduate course. I was interested to see if the trainee's age, maturity, experience and competence had any significant affect upon the relationship. Having completed the interview I then asked the staff about the children's personal situation at home so that their pattern of family experience could be taken into account.

Of course there was the difficulty of presenting the questions to the children without prejudicing the responses. How was I, an adult male unknown to the children, to gain that honest insight into their feelings? Their experience of men might affect their responses; my appearance as an outsider could restrict their openness. In fact the children were remarkably frank and forthright, though understandably their behaviour tended to reflect the ethos and culture of the school. Some were quiet and needed greater encouragement, others were full of opinions and recounted in glorious detail what had happened. None of them appeared to have any concern about my tape recorder, probably because such items are too common to cause any comment today. Several were anxious to ensure that what they said would 'not have my name on it'. The questions I asked had to be neutrally phrased to avoid emphasizing that I was exploring gender difference, which I interpreted as 'social, cultural and psychological aspects linked to males and females through particular social contexts'.

Many of the children greeted the news of the arrival of a male trainee with great excitement mixed with some anxiety, especially from the older girls. I asked them,

> What did you expect when you learnt that you were to have Mr Denby?
> We thought he would be shouty and strict.
> Unsure what to expect . . . thrilled.
> We were not sure because we had never had a man teacher.
> Men are more tough than ladies.
> We thought – oh no!

Several expressed their feeling very bluntly:

> We were surprised, normally it didn't matter.
> He would certainly be different from a female.

Some Year 6 girls had a rather jaundiced view of the boys in their class; they paused and then one said:

> Mainly boys are naughty but if he uses the teacher's system he will be all right.

Some boys had their worries too, expecting life to become more serious, but generally they were positive:

> Yes! – a man.
> Good, a change, a different environment.

Boys in another school thought that it would be a nice change and very fair and not sexist, although one of them said, perhaps more honestly:

> Great . . . a new teacher . . . that means easy work for a while.

For many children a new face is a welcome change, particularly in the smaller schools. Any new pattern of working relationship may well have some initial success. Understandably when asked, they tended to compare their recent experience with previous (almost universally female) trainee placements:

> She was just like miss, he did new things.
> Usually it's *just* ladies.

It almost seems as though male trainees may have an unfair advantage here simply because of their novelty value. Often children did appear to pay more attention to them and did want to please them. Presumably this may well have vanished if the trainee had been with them for a longer period. However it is not always an advantage as in the case of an infant boy reporting:

> He was easy to control ... he was not used to children.

The comment was substantiated by the class teacher agreeing that the third-year trainee had yet to gain sufficient personal confidence to be suitably severe with the children. Boys in various schools have said to me that they see their male trainee as a big brother rather than as a teacher or father figure and a common problem that males experience early in their training to be a teacher is in establishing that role difference. It has to originate in their own self-image of themselves as 'teachers'. Some have this before they come to college but many have to develop the appropriate character and inner-confidence once they have begun working with children within schools. Speaking with male trainees I have been aware that they often choose to specialize as upper-junior teachers because that is the age group that they feel most at home with, to the extent that several recognized the Peter Pan analogy, 'leading younger children through an exciting world of discovery and challenge, where no-one ever grew older'.

Is there anything wrong with wanting to work within an environment in which you feel comfortable and appreciated?

The combined effect of a low proportion of male teachers in school, the tendency for those present commonly to be based in the upper-junior classes and the diminishing number of male trainees does mean that many pupils have no prior experience of being taught by a man. So when a young male trainee does appear in the classroom it can be a novel event. Almost always the children were understandably anxious beforehand:

> We thought that he would be loud.

> Men get angry and shout.

> Men are aggressive, it would be stricter.

One child in an all-female staffed school said how she kept on thinking about the Dunblane tragedy, and having a man walking around would make her frightened. More commonly they said that the knowledge that a man was going to be in school was comforting, paradoxically this included a junior girl in a small community whose violent father had left home and whose teenage brother had been imprisoned for assault. There were several indications that children looked to the male trainee for protection and to manage certain tasks:

> We haven't got any men here so he could deal with the tramp that hangs around the rec.

> We won't have to wait to get the balls off the roof.

A lower-junior boy simply felt more secure with a man in the school. Some of these expectations may be unrealistic yet they do indicate the sublimated beliefs that may prevail and within which the trainee must function.

I asked each group of children to tell me about something they had really enjoyed doing whilst Mr X has been working in their class. In response most groups listed a predictable range of activities and subjects, though the imaginative events stood out:

> He tried to teach us juggling and skipping [drama time in a circus], he joined in, it was a laugh!

> He really enjoyed the subjects – so we did. He made us think more brainier.

> We enjoyed the new subjects ... he got us to look at the stars ... and to go running.

> We used the computer to do some really special art work for sports day.

When asked how easy had it been to work with Mr X a frequent comment had been that he had explained things well:

> He didn't shout, he was patient, so we can understand.

> He made things clear for us, unlike the female student we had last time.

> His young interests helped, (referring to pop-music and football teams).

The trainee's trust in children was important, especially to the boys:

> He trusted us to behave ... so we did.

> He gave us free choice of seating and we enjoyed that independence and trust ... we worked for him.

Some of the most forthright responses came from a group of Year 2 children in a typical Victorian red-brick city-centre school:

> He was always cheerful, didn't shout as much as our teacher ... so we behaved better for him.

> We acted differently [they behaved well] ... because we knew he was going soon.

Significantly it was often the quality of the relationship that was important to both boys and girls, mutual respect and fun, that assisted all aspects of the placements.

Reflect upon your own experience of memorable/formative teachers that you have known; in what ways and to what extent was their gender significant to that fruitful relationship?

The identification of patience and trust as two common characteristics was a point identified by an inner-city head who had noticed those aspects in other male trainees, although his analysis was not complimentary. 'Men want to keep in with the pupils, and they are not sure how young children will respond, that is why they are soft'. Male trainees' lack of familiarity with children is an assumption that many teachers make without any attempt to ascertain the truth . Any hesitance may be due to their anxiety not to be accused of being abusive or their natural politeness rather than any indecisiveness.

One of my questions asked the children if anything they had done with Mr X had been a bit special or different? Interestingly only one group mentioned an activity that might have been thought of as 'typically male', in an all-female school a man had extended their games repertoire. That is not to say that the trainees were simply replicating the class teacher's practice. Many pupils said that the trainee was greatly valued:

> He made everything fun.

> His fun way of introducing things, he asked us to help him remember things ... like sending the dinner register back on time.

> He really enjoyed the subjects.

With many of the interviews children had reported that there were some differences in the male trainee's approach:

> He was more consistent.

> He'd listen to us and let us finish what we had to say.

> He was easier to talk to.

> He was always positive.

It was with the four mature male trainees in particular that children commented very positively upon the even-handed way that they had been managed, how they had been respected and treated with fairness:

> Lady teachers tell boys off more than girls.

> Women [teachers] pick on the boys ... so we respond by being nasty to the girls.

Top junior girls at one school said that life was fairer with a male teacher:

> You [all] need someone of your own sort to talk to, someone to share your ideas with.

I asked this group would it have mattered if it had been Mr Inman rather than Mrs Squires when you wanted personal advice about any problem you had at home or at school:

> Not really, so long as you know they are listening and not thinking about something else.

> Mr Inman always had time to listen.

To my surprise it was with a group of seven-year-old children who had regular experience of teachers of both sexes that the most bald statement was made by a young boy, who already knew he wanted to be a lawyer:

> Boy teachers and girl teachers are nearly the same, but their attitudes are different.

His expressed opinion echoed through my findings. It was clear that there was a widespread perceived sense of fairness in the way that male trainees operated. Now 'fairness' is a constructed concept and does not in itself guarantee any advantages; what is seen as *fair* to one party may be clearly *unfair* to another. The development of any global sense of equality of opportunity and entitlement may be a facet of true maturity and one that many adults fail to grasp, yet its initial formation can begin very early in a child's life given the right stimuli.

Suggestions for:

Further reading

Biddulph, S. (1994) *Manhood*, London: Hawthorn Press.
   Steve Biddulph presents a philosophy of life for males, as children, adults and fathers. He maintains that men need to re-discover the skills by which they can positively influence future generations.
Raphael Reed, L. (1999) 'Troubling boys and disturbing discourses on masculinity and schooling: A feminist exploration of current debates and interventions concerning boys in school', *Gender and Education* 11(1): 93–110.
   Some elements of a feminist's perspective on masculinity and schooling are developed.
Skelton, C. (1998) Feminism and Research into Masculinities and Schooling, *Gender and Education* 10(2): 217–27.
   Christine Skelton regularly publishes stimulating articles on sexual identity and its acquisition, drawing upon her extensive work within primary schools.
Thornton, M. (1999) 'Men into primary teaching: Who goes where?', *Education 3–13* 27(2): 50–56.
   Mary has been involved with a large-scale research programme examining the training and employment of men entering the teaching profession, with particular regard to their career development.
   The journal *Gender and Education* regularly has many articles developing our awareness of issues of great importance in this area.

18 'Miss, why are you brown?'

Some children's perceptions of black and Asian trainee teachers in 'all-white' schools

Charles Batteson

Introduction

This chapter explores some of the ways in which children in predominantly or wholly white primary schools perceive and respond to black and Asian trainee teachers. How might constructions of 'race' and 'ethnicity' affect the ways in which white children interact with and respond to black and Asian trainees? The study is based on a number of small-scale case studies, studies that offer us insights on children's perceptions of individuals, in this case teachers, who 'look' different. I link these observations about race and ethnicity to children's more general reflections about trainee teachers.

Over the past twenty years a great deal has been written and spoken about the desirability of recruiting more 'ethnic minority' individuals into the teaching profession. Part of this hinges on a desire to reflect the multicultural nature of British society, part on a quest for social cohesiveness and justice. There are frequent references to the possibility that black and Asian teachers could become positive role models demonstrating to ethnic minority children that educational success is possible. For schools with a predominantly white intake, it is held that a more diverse teaching profession would properly reflect the current nature of society. However, to date, there has been only limited progress in enhancing ethnic minority teacher recruitment. In part this is due to persisting underachievement amongst not only blacks and Asians but also the working-class community so that entrance rates to higher education, including teacher training, are lower than for those from more advantaged backgrounds. Those who do go on to college or university are reluctant to consider a career in teaching, preferring options which appear to have higher status and greater financial prospects.

Within the population of ethnic minority teacher trainees there are some distinct patterns. A 1998 survey (Teacher Training Agency/Commission for Racial Equality 1998) indicated that ethnic minority trainees were more likely to be mature entrants, clustered in predominantly urban, multicultural locations and attending institutions near their homes. This means that in many training institutions and geographical areas there are very few ethnic minority trainees. While there has been useful research on classroom and teaching experiences in the relatively few areas where ethnic minority trainees are clustered (Osler 1997, Jones and Maguire 1997) we know little about the experience and impact of trainees who undertake their training in predominantly white, greenfield or rural locations. Often, having a black or Asian student teaching in their classroom is the first direct, person-to-person experience that white children have of any black, Asian or ethnic minority individuals. This is the context in which to explore the ways in which children, and indeed teachers and parents, perceive and respond to such encounters. It allows us to revisit some of our assumptions about children's views on race and ethnicity and to discuss more general observations about child/trainee relationships within broader initial teacher training processes.

The material for this study was drawn from semi-structured conversations with children in primary schools in wholly or predominantly white areas. It is supplemented by interviews with Asian and black (Afro-Caribbean) trainee teachers, their supervising teacher mentors and headteachers. There is reference to a case where an Asian trainee completed a long-term teaching placement in a school with a majority of Asian pupils. This involved some surprises that challenge certain stereotypes. The need to call into question certain taken-for-granted assumptions is a theme which runs through this account; it is based on what children actually said. A 'case study' approach lends itself to changes of partiality. Hopefully these are redeemed by parallel advantages deriving from authenticity – that no claims are made beyond those being voiced by participants.

Possible explanations of children's perceptions and attitudes towards race and ethnicity necessarily go beyond this specific inquiry. In the past some educationalists had rather romantic and perhaps naive views of children's innocence and intrinsic goodwill; some educational research endorses this position. We need to be reminded that exploring children's views towards race and ethnicity is sensitive. Over twenty years ago Jeffcoate (1977) indicated that even very young (nursery-aged) children may be adept at telling adults what they think we want to know and hear rather than what the children really believe. Similarly, Gaine (1995) has graphically illustrated some of the pitfalls arising from uncritically accepting what he labels a 'no problem here' approach. This accepts the proposition that in white areas children will have no preferred views on race and will not have negative or hostile attitudes. That colour-blind approach has often been affirmed and even celebrated in predominantly white primary schools. However it significantly underestimates and often ignores the influence of parents, families, communities and, crucially, the mass media on children's imagery and mind-sets. Thus when white children first encounter black or Asian individuals socially – in this case as student teachers – they have an indication to be variously positively or negatively disposed. The influences and consequences of such mind-sets, came through in some of the following narratives.

First impressions

The initial idea for this chapter stemmed from informal conversations with two student teachers (Victoria Thomas and Pauveen Mimza).

Victoria describes herself as 'Afro-Caribbean'. She completed her second last block placement in an 'all white' rural primary school, St Bede's, located in a small village twenty-five miles from the nearest urban centre. Pauveen describes herself as 'Asian of Indian origin'. Her final practice was in a large city primary school, Harrison Road, where 435 of the 480 children were of Asian (largely Bangladeshi) origin.

Mrs James, the headteacher, commented that Victoria was 'the first black person that virtually any of the children will have met face to face'. On her first visit to the school Victoria recollected that she was an object of fascination: 'They seemed to find me exotic. There was a lot of interest in me, not just from my class but from all the other children in the school'. Mrs Johnson (Victoria's mentor) described the children's obvious interest as being 'innocent and positive and something that she built on and used to good effect over the ten weeks'. Both thought the children were awe-struck by Victoria's Birmingham accent as well as her colour. The children described Victoria as a 'good teacher', 'kind and caring', 'not as strict as she was at first'. They had no hesitation in discussing their first encounters with a black person and in talking about different ethnic groups and life styles. Victoria herself, in retrospect, felt the initial 'exotic impression' soon developed as a positive feature. Mrs Johnson concurred: 'The children wanted to do well for her. They're an eager and busy class and were even more so for her. They were fascinated by her colour and hair but this wasn't hostile. In a sense she was a human learning resource – bringing into the school a part of society which our children had never encountered'. Victoria had worked in three other 'all white', small town/suburban schools where the children had passing/partial acquaintances with other ethnic groups. She was struck by the powerful initial impression her presence had on children and was initially apprehensive. However, she thought her visual 'difference' and 'uniqueness' were powerful factors in developing a highly positive rapport. Children accommodated themselves.

Pauveen's experiences were something of a culture shock. She had been born, grown up and educated in a 'small, prosperous, middle-class town' (in the Home Counties). The Bengali children in Harrison Road were surprised that she could neither speak nor understand their mother tongue, as were some parents and other Asian members of staff. While Victoria's blackness in an entirely white school was a positive feature Pauveen had to contend with stereotypical assumptions. In terms of both language and culture she was seen as different from children with whom on the surface she appeared to share ethnic affinities. She and Miss Howe (her mentor) observed that this led children to be bemused and sometimes confused. Nominal ethnic origin was less important than social and cultural background. There are dangers inherent in labelling individuals and pitfalls in assuming that black and Asian teachers ought to be role models or cultural ambassadors.

The experiences of Victoria and Pauveen prompted my more systematic exploration of some of these issues. This was conducted with the cooperation and agreement of two Asian students, Gurjit Virdee and Sunita Siraj.

Gurjit

Gurjit is 22, was born and grew up in Leicester, attended an 'All Asian' primary school and a 'multicultural' secondary school. She describes her own primary and secondary education as 'good, lively and encouraging ambition'. She contrasted the prevalence of optimism and anticipation of success that she encountered with a tendency of despair and hopelessness that seemed to inhabit the areas where she was on teaching practice. Gurjit completed a ten-week teaching practice in an urban Roman Catholic primary school. St Aloysius serves a run-down, severely disadvantaged neighbourhood. While the city has a significant Pakistani community, the estate where most of St Aloysius's children live is predominantly white. Of 240 children the school roll identifies only six as ethnic minority (four Asians, two mixed-race). Gurjit had a Year 2 class of six and seven year olds. She describes herself as Asian (of Indian origin).

After her pre-practice visit to St Aloysius school Gurjit was apprehensive. About a third of the houses in the catchment estate were vacant – boarded up and extensively vandalized. Graphically racist slogans were daubed on the walls. St Aloysius school itself is a 1930s red-brick single floor building laid out along two inter-connected corridors. It contains two separate primary schools, one Roman Catholic, St Aloysius, and Alderman Ramsey school which is non-denominational and LEA maintained. The head was a man, the nine teachers were women. All were white, and eight of the ten had grown up within a thirty-mile radius of the school.

Gurjit was introduced as 'a new teacher who will be joining us for most of next term'. On her planning/preparatory visits she observed the whole class of twenty-seven (all white) children, spoke to some of them individually and in groups, and was given her teaching schedule. The class-teacher, mid-way through the second week of Gurjit's ten-week placement, said that she was anxious that the overt racism expressed by the graffiti on the walls of the estate might represent the attitudes of some children and their parents towards her. Gurjit experienced no racist prejudice, overt or shadowy, herself but some staff members reported that an Asian boy in Year 6 was frequently the target of bullying at playtimes which involved explicitly racist name calling. The school responds to this within its whole-school behaviour policy.

Gurjit felt that Miss Howe's (her mentor) initial introduction of her to the class was important: her status as a new/different teacher was clearly valued. On a previous placement she'd been introduced as a student and felt this lessened her credibility amongst children. From the outset of her practice her confidence increased. She received positive feedback and a highly positive assessment from Miss Howe. At the end of the practice she remembered two specific remarks relating to race/ethnicity. In her first week, Nadine asked during a playtime: 'Miss, why are you brown?'. Gurjit replied 'I'm an Asian woman. My mum and dad came to England from a country called India, almost everybody there is a brown colour just like me.' Gurjit felt that Nadine was satisfied with this explanation. Towards the end of the day, Gurjit briefly returned to the 'why are you brown?' question. Without mentioning Nadine by name, she repeated the question to the class. Some of the children's responses included: 'You come from a hot country', 'You come from Pakistan', 'You come from Stafford Street' (in a fairly near, predominantly Asian part of the city). Gurjit described the brief discussion as 'matter of fact, very down to earth'. She wasn't convinced that pointing out either Leicester or India on a map had much meaning for the children and pondered on whether this had confused rather than informed them.

Gurjit overheard one of the mothers, towards the end of her second week say 'At least this one hasn't got an accent'. (Gurjit describes her accent as 'standard English with just a hint of a Leicester accent creeping in'.) In a conversation about this with Miss Howe, Gurjit decided that the comparison referred to a supply teacher – an Asian woman – who'd taught the children for a term the year before. Gurjit and Miss Howe both felt that parents became increasingly warmly disposed towards her as they met at the beginning and end of the school day. Miss Howe felt that the children's enthusiastic reports about their work with Gurjit were repeated to their parents who accepted her as a 'good', 'proper' teacher. Miss Howe thought both children and parents 'treated Gurjit just like they treat me', that is as an 'authentic teacher'.

Individually and in groups the children displayed various perceptions of race. Shaun's first impression of Gurjit was 'that she was brown'. Anthony's that 'she was brown like Miss Kaur . . . because they're coloured they're a bit strict. They're OK though.' Louise noted the 'brownness' as somewhat unusual ''cause we haven't got any brown people in Class 2'. Ashley linked Gurjit with his own experience: 'She's coloured. All of my street is full of coloured people. I like them very much because they always share things with us.' Ashley's family had moved from the local estate because of the violence and vandalism. They lived in a small terraced house in an adjacent 'Asian area'. The various favourable and neutral comments on 'colour' or 'brownness' expressed by children seem partly to stem from their greater vivid anxiety about violent local white gangs and neighbours. Nadine described her fears about 'Shona's mum, she's a real tough girl, she's even hit my mum and dad'. Anthony described how he now lived in 'a black area'. His family moved from the estate because they 'got burgled twice ... people pick on you ... you couldn't go into your own garden because people like Shaun and Amy – they're eleven – would come and bully you'. The tension in the school neighbourhood and the fear of violence were apparent amongst many of the children in Gurjit's class. The bordering 'black/Asian' locality was perceived as safer and more desirable. While their school was an almost entirely white school, some of the children had direct and positive personal experience of black/Asian people. This may have informed their initial and ongoing positive response to Gurjit. Her class responses ranged from the openly quizzical ('why are you brown') to a matter-of-fact routiness of being near (and sometimes living amongst) black/brown people.

While the class of six and seven year olds came to like and respect Gurjit she had to earn this. The children's criteria for her being adjudged a 'good' teacher hinged on many of the factors outlined in previous chapters.

Sunita Siraj

Sunita is 22 and describes herself as 'Asian and a Hindu'. She was born and grew up in a suburb of Manchester where she attended primary and secondary schools which she recalled as 'about half Asian and half white'.

Sunita completed a ten-week placement at the same time as Gurjit. Manor Way LEA Primary School was less than a mile away from St Aloysius. The 270 children mostly live on the surrounding council estate. The architecture and layout are similar but this estate has been substantially improved. Most of the small terrace and semi-detached houses have been gutted and re-fitted over the past six years. Few are vacant. There is very little of graffiti or litter. The catchment area is predominantly white. The school estimates that fifteen of its children are of ethnic minority origin (Asian, Afro-Caribbean and mixed race). Aiyshah (a Year 4 pupil) remarked that 'all the Muslims in the school are my cousins'. By way of contrast another adjacent school, some mile and a half distant was described by Sunita's headteacher, Mr Farrow, as 'about 97 per cent Asian with about three quarters having English as an additional language'.

Sunita had a positive feeling about the school after her preparatory visits. The 1930s single-tier building, laid out on a triangular pattern, was 'well decorated, bright and welcoming'. Though some of the children manifested behavioural problems most seemed amenable and well motivated.

Sunita was introduced to her Year 4 class, and thereafter generally referred to by staff and children, as 'a student'. This seemed to influence some initial and ongoing perceptions. Michael commented: 'We've had loads of students, all different. We had Miss Medhu [also Asian], she helped Mr Smith with the display.' Fiona noted that 'Miss Siraj is a student like Miss Nelson and Miss Medhu. They only come in on Tuesdays.' These perceptions of student teachers as intermittent helpers rather than qualified teachers seemed to militate against her acceptance by the class as a 'proper' teacher. Sunita felt that her class-teacher/mentor, Mr Taylor, was reluctant to allow her to assume a fuller range of responsibilities until nearly half way through her placement. He was also the maths coordinator but devolved little real responsibility in this area. He had been very direct in discussing Sunita's ethnic identity with her and how the children might respond towards her: 'I don't think you'll experience much in the way of racism from the children. They're familiar with local Asian people and seem generally to get on with them.' But he warned that 'the biggest problem here is loutish-laddish-behaviour amongst our Year 5 and 6 boys', and explained that this was the reason the afternoon playtime had been abolished. The school had also developed a system involving a high level of supervision and structured activities during lunch times as a means to counter this negative behaviour. Sunita did not witness or experience any racist incidents during her teaching practice. Initially she had been concerned with the hostile responses towards her from Colin a mixed-race boy in her class. However this didn't appear to be racially motivated but symptomatic of a rather wider problem. Colin explained that: 'I don't like my mum, I don't like my dad. I don't like school.' Perhaps more significantly he recalled that, at the start of her placement: 'Sunita didn't shout at us like Mr Smith does. But she does now! Men are strict, ladies aren't, if they're not strict they can't be good teachers.'

Sunita had been asked to prepare an RE topic on Hinduism. This was an opportunity for her and the children to discuss formally her own ethnic and religious identity and to relate this to her teaching. Sunita was pleased to be able to develop a substantial piece of work on her own, drawing on both her main college subject and personal experience. As the children discussed the topic they also offered some insights into their images of ethnicity and culture. (A sort of elongated version of Gurjit's 'Miss, why are you brown?'.) Their often positive and enthusiastic response to the study on Hinduism seemed partly to derive from favourable and positive images of Asian communities and neighbourhoods in other parts of the city. Although their own school and estate were over-whelmingly white, Sunita's class had something of a world- (or at least a city-wide) view. Thus: 'There's lots of Hindus, they live near the park – the one near the Spar shop. They're really nice people and they don't fall out.' Again: Neil (Year 4) 'In (city) there's people like us [white] and there are those brown Hindu people. And they're friendly and they've got kids. When they go by they go like that [Neil gesticulates the Hindu namase greeting].'

Of note was the fact that a locally prominent ethnic minority group was categorized by religion (Hindu) rather than by race (Asian/'brown'). This was in marked contrast to the operational definitions expressed by children in Gurjit's class (remembering the schools are within a mile of each other). This may reflect the different RE policies of the two schools. Manor Way, Sunita's school, had an explicit focus on 'world religions'. Her work on Hinduism was clearly within this policy and was seen by children as a routine event. That is not to say Sunita's self-identity was not visible or influential. Christopher proudly explained 'Our teacher's a Hindu. She told us so!' A group of six children powerfully agreed with Aiyshah's view: 'All of our class have learned a lot about Hinduism. It's fun learning about Hinduism because Miss Siraj is a Hindu.' They also concurred with Wesley's praiseworthy remark: 'She's done a wonderful Hinduism [display] board'. The children seemed to value the range and volume of material and artefacts which Sunita brought to class: 'She makes it good fun, you can dress up and touch all the artefacts' (Paul). Cathy concurred: 'We usually dress up, or one of us dresses up and the others can hold things [artefacts]'. The practical hands-on way Sunita presented Hinduism was a key factor in the children's learning. Kelsey, a child with significant learning difficulties, could freely recall: 'Hindus can cut things with these sharp plants. They wear long, colourful dresses. Muslims and Hindus are not the same thing. Hindus have temples. Muslims have Mosques.'

Sunita's class were positively disposed towards her. Her personal identity and the ways she exploited this within a specific curriculum area contributed to, but did not solely account for, her being perceived as a credible teacher. That stemmed from more general comments: 'She's a nice girl'; 'She doesn't yell at people'; 'She's kind and she doesn't yell at you straight away'; 'She doesn't give you lines'. A 'kind' collective disposition depended on Sunita's overall pedagogic performance; the children's already positive perceptions of other 'Hindu people' whom they knew from casual, intermittent encounters in the city; and the up-front ethos of the school: to promote knowledge and tolerance of different people and cultures. The opportunities for Sunita to use the work on Hinduism were part and parcel of a whole-school approach, not an exotic, pragmatic tokenistic interlude.

The children responded to Sunita in a very matter-of-fact way. Their evaluations rested substantially on her overall classroom competence ('having discipline', 'coming to us straight away when we put our hand up', 'not yelling', 'not giving lines'). Children had clearly defined models of what a teacher ought to be and do, and Sunita reflected those models. They related well to Sunita, acknowledged and were positive towards her ethnicity and, particularly her religion. This partly stemmed from partial acquaintance and knowledge of other, local 'Hindu' people.

Conclusion

The small-scale study on which this chapter is based indicates that in areas of racial/cultural awareness children are sometimes highly inquisitive. Their explicitness reveals often positive dispositions towards black and Asian trainee teachers and communities. These are in addition to well-defined models used to perceive 'proper', 'real' teachers. There are further implications for preparing carefully for initial and early encounters between all trainees and the children they will be working with. In offering children an understanding of the multicultural society in which they will grow up and live it is insufficient (and unfair) to delegate responsibility to black and Asian 'role models'. Children may demonstrate an explicit willingness to engage with, discuss and learn about social and cultural diversity far and above some of our expectations.

Postscript

This chapter was written in the immediate aftermath of the Macpherson Report on the murder of Stephen Lawrence, a black teenager killed in South London in 1993. Public debate focused on the extent of institutional racism including its impact on education. Much ensuing discussion was formidably depressing. However some of Gurjit and Sunita's experiences may offer a counter-balance to the completeness of doom and gloom scenarios.

References

Gaine, C. (1995) *Still No Problem Here*, Stoke-on-Trent: Trentham.

Jeffcoate, R. (1977) 'Children's racial ideas and feelings', *English in Education* 11(1): 32–48.

Jones, C. and Maguire, M. (1997) 'Before, during and after: being black and doing a P.G.C.E.', paper presented at the British Educational Research Association Annual Conference, York, September.

Osler, A. (1997) *The Education and Careers of Black Teachers: Changing identities, changing lives*, Buckingham: Open University Press.

Teacher Training Agency/Commission for Racial Equality (1998) *Teaching in Multi-Ethnic Britain: A Joint Report*, London: TTA/CRE.

Afterword

Marion Blake and Florence Samson

Connections and new beginnings

I (Marion Blake) am a Canadian. I have lived in England for seven years, the last five working in London as a freelance editor. Previously I had studied at the London University Institute of Education and then been involved in initial teacher training in the Ontario Institute for Studies in Education at the University of Toronto. I was delighted to use both these aspects of my experience when Hilary Cooper and Rob Hyland invited me to work with them in liaising with this team of tutors from St Martin's College to write up their project on Children's Perceptions of Learning with Trainee Teachers as a book. I gained further insight into current developments in teacher education in England. These provided much food for discussion, during e-mails and late-night telephone calls with my old friend and colleague Florence Samson who still works at OISE (the Ontario Institute for Studies in Education). Indeed Florence now has responsibility for partnerships between schools and the Toronto Institute.

When I told Hilary and Rob about my chats with Florence they suggested I write them as the afterword to the book, since there seem to be so many parallels between Ontario and the UK; in regulating teaching programmes; increasing demands on students and teachers, who are nevertheless expected to continue to reflect on their practice, and to give of themselves, within the new partnership arrangements. They felt that this might put the book into a wider context.

So, to conclude, readers are welcome to share, and join in, some of my late-night telephone exchanges with Florence.

Marion Dear Florence, your phone call was a lifesaver. I couldn't figure out a way to get started and all my 'how to write' advice that I've passed out so freely and often to all and sundry wasn't doing me a blind bit of good. And there was Jerome Bruner reminding me that conversations with friends was one of the most important and constant forms of drafts of any writing he does.

Florence Yes, I agree. And conversations have been reality and metaphor ever since we met. I think that was about ten years ago in the Joint Centre for Teacher Development office? Mick [Mick Connelly, head of the centre] introduced us, term hadn't started yet and I was really happy to meet an old hand.

Marion Old hand indeed. I'd been around the tenth floor of OISE a lot when I was a research officer on Gordon Wells' big language in schools project, and sort of drifted along to Mick to start my PhD. I think that was the summer I was working on the Lawrence Stenhouse section of Mick and Jean's [Jean Clandinin] chapter on teachers as curricular makers for ... ?? Florence do you remember the name of the book?

Florence Curriculum makers is a nice phrase but it seems to me that here at the University of Toronto and in Ontario generally we – people like me who teach education courses, provincial government through its policies and prescriptions, the new Ontario College of Teachers which regulates teachers and preservice programmes – seem to leave little room for curriculum making practitioners.

Marion Yes, the names of the official bodies are different but the intentions and demands sound very much alike. One of the tacit, sometimes explicit, themes in the book is that student teachers should devise ways to 'reflect on their practice', particularly from their pupils' perspectives. How do they find the time? How do *you* help them to develop this skill? How do you help them to make links between their practice and theory?

Florence Well every student has three general assignments in addition to the requirements of their subject speciality lecturers. One of these is an action research project in the Spring-Term practicum (five weeks) some present their projects at the annual OISE Action Research Conference.

Marion Sounds like a book in itself. Did this in some way come out of the Action Research Conference in Manchester? I've been trying to remember the topic of our presentation. OK, try me with the other two.

Florence Each student has to develop an integrated curriculum unit, since the Central Option has as its focus the integration of the various subject areas.

Marion That's really startling, because I remember when we all looked to Britain as the home of all those wonderful term-long projects that integrated everything. Now, of course, with the way the National Curriculum for each subject is being interpreted, the subjects seem to be more discrete. Lots of comment in the press as well as the education journals, but as you'll see when you read the book that isn't necessarily true in classrooms. Lorna Crossman for example, shows how trainee teachers bring Religious Education to life, through music, singing, dance, movement and art. Kevin Hamel describes a case study in which music is taught through Information Technology. Indeed Liz Elliott and Pete Saunders show how ICT can be an integral part of subjects across the curriculum. And in Science Anne Riggs and Aftab Gujral actively encourage trainees to record science investigation through art, embroidery and drama. What about the third assignment?

Florence A portfolio. This is a record of professional accomplishments, and always of work in progress. Students choose what they will include and are encouraged to see it as an on-going record, a way of noting gaps. At the end of the second semester students present their portfolios to a team of instructors. We question them about why they included certain items – their reasons are more important than the 'dazzle them with colour' aspect of the physical portfolio. I found this to be one of the highlights of the year – a real sense of students 'becoming' professional teachers. We also think this will be useful when they go for job interviews. Maybe we could think about helping the students to weave in children's perspectives a bit more through . . .

Marion As part of this expanded CV? Sounds like a great idea to me. You probably won't be surprised to know that one of my soap boxes continues to be the unfairness of research carried out by academics. Without the teachers there wouldn't be any research to report and yet, because of some outmoded convention, teachers are not allowed to use their real names in the published work. Well, good for Mick [Michael Connelly, Marion's PhD supervisor] he agreed that Ann Maher would be Ann Maher in my thesis.

I'm remembering our favourite Madeleine Grumet quote 'we bring our names, our histories, our promises'. Seems to me this fits in with what you're doing and is certainly a given in several of the chapters in this book – Jill Pemberton on art, Lorna Crossman on religious education, it shines through all the chapters really.

Florence Yes, and we've had some good times thinking and writing about the implications of that phrase. At the first meeting of the Teacher Education seminar (intended to give the students a chance to synthesize what they're learning in the practicum and in the university lectures), I ask them to write a page on what teaching means to them and why they've chosen this profession. In April I ask them the same questions.

I take a similar approach in my Social Studies class. As you know, I believe we teach who we are and our life experience enters the classroom with us, our beliefs and values, our biases and prejudices. I ask the students to think of the influences in their lives and the direction they have now decided on. At the end of the year we go back to this assignment.

Marion Sounds as though there are a lot of conversations going on?

Florence Yes, although as usual there's never enough time. Faxes, e-mail and phone calls – couldn't do without them. But there's nothing like a live conversation, the pauses and intonations help me to pull in the threads that remain invisible on the e-mail screen. Print on screen and paper doesn't excite and inspire me in the same way.

Marion Yes, there were times when I longed to sit down with the chapter authors so we could explain what we *really* meant. As it turned out, I think they have done a great job in discussing their work at a distance with someone they don't know at all. Probably some surprises when we finally meet. I really can't believe that Hilary and I have never met!

I realize that in the expanding partnership arrangements here, more and more is expected of the classroom teachers who accept student teachers, I think they're often called mentors. What's happening in Ontario?

Florence In Ontario they have the title Associate Teacher and they are one hundred per cent responsible for evaluating the student teacher's practicum. This is carried out half way into the practicum, the student completes an identical self-evaluation form, and a course of action is decided on.

Marion Any prospects of getting a more equal balance of responsibility and resources? What do you think about UK proposals for a fast-track route to responsibility, schemes for paying top salaries to super teachers and 'payment by results' which is being floated by the DfEE?

Florence It's too late at night to begin *that* conversation.

Marion Florence, did I tell you that Jessica [Marion's ten-year-old granddaughter who lives in Ottawa] has started in a brand new school? The big excitement on the first day was that they all gathered in front of the new school to have their picture taken by a photographer who was up on a fire truck extension ladder. I have been thinking of all the people directly mentioned in this book and imagining them gathered for an aerial photograph. And of course I'd want to include all those individual indispensable people who have shaped our history and recognized our promise. To begin? Connie Rosen, Anne Oakley, Clifford Geertz, David Booth, Jimmy Britton, Donald Graves – and so may more. I'll send you the book just as soon as it's out; I don't know if there'll be a photo . . .

Index

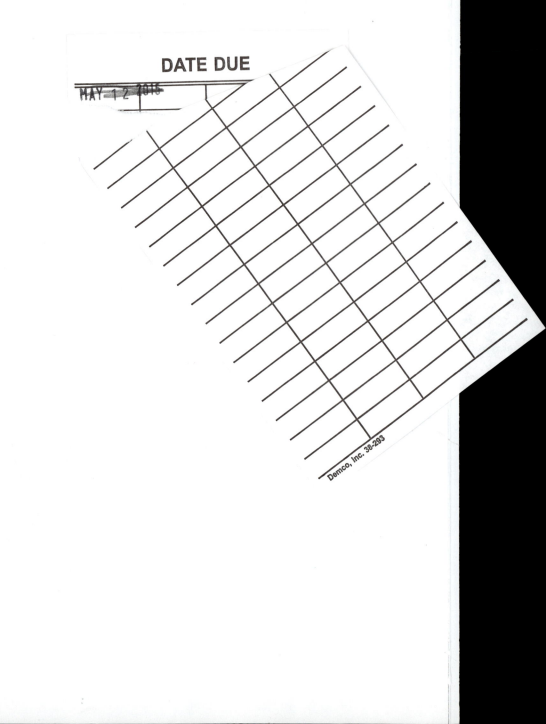

DATE DUE

MAY 1 2 2015

Demco, Inc. 38-293